As a head coach you are always looking for opportunities to build team chemistry. In *How to Be the Ultimate Teammate*, Pat Williams cites many great lessons on how to become the "ultimate teammate." By adhering to these lessons, you will eventually build the kind of team chemistry needed to be a winner. Pat has beautifully intertwined the lessons of sports with the lessons of life—lessons that I believe we should all follow, especially the lessons regarding "service to others." I am grateful to Pat for giving me the opportunity to read this book and learn to better myself as a husband, father, brother, son, and friend, as well as a coach.

Ron Rivera
Head Coach
Carolina Panthers

Pat Williams, through all of his experiences building winning teams, has gained incredible insights into what it takes to become an impactful teammate. Pat shares 15 proven strategies that will guide readers to lead themselves and, in turn, their teammates.

Jim Caldwell
Head Coach
Detroit Lions

Pat Williams is one of the very best in his profession, and the 15 lessons he has outlined in *How to Be the Ultimate Teammate* should be required reading for anyone who is part of a team. It doesn't matter whether it's a sports team or business team, these lessons will help you become a better person and teammate—which could make the difference between being good or being the best.

George O'Leary
Head Football Coach
University of Central Florida

D11128785

HOW TO BE
THE ULTIMATE TEAMMATE

PAT WILLIAMS
WITH JIM DENNEY

ISBN: 978-1-60679-307-7
Library of Congress Control Number: 2014940167
Cover design: Cheery Sugabo
Book layout: Cheery Sugabo
Front cover photos: Fuse/Thinkstock

Coaches Choice
P.O. Box 1828
Monterey, CA 93942
www.coaceschoice.com

DEDICATION

This book is dedicated to Jameer Nelson, a great competitor and an outstanding role model for teammates everywhere.

ACKNOWLEDGMENTS

With deep appreciation, I acknowledge the support and guidance of the following people who helped make this book possible:

Special thanks to Alex Martins, Dan DeVos, and Rich DeVos of the Orlando Magic.

Hats off to my associate Andrew Herdliska; my proofreader, Ken Hussar; and my ace typist, Fran Thomas.

Thanks also to my writing partner, Jim Denney, for his superb contributions in shaping this manuscript.

Hearty thanks also go to Jim Peterson, Kristi Huelsing, Angie Perry, and the entire Coaches Choice team for their vision and insight, and for believing that we had something important to say in these pages.

And, finally, special thanks and appreciation go to my wife, Ruth, and to my wonderful and supportive family. They are truly the backbone of my life.

FOREWORD

It's a well-worn cliché: "Sports is a metaphor for life."

I say sports is a metaphor for what this world *could* and *should* be. Team sports is about people from different backgrounds, classes, races, religions, and points of view all coming together, merging their strengths and abilities to achieve one goal: *Winning*.

In a team environment, every player must set aside ego, selfishness, laziness, and exhaustion. Every player must say, "I choose to unselfishly relinquish my personal wants and needs, and even my rights, in order to be 100 percent committed to my teammates."

Our teammates come first. Nothing matters but the success of the team. When players learn to put "team" ahead of "self," incredible things happen. The whole becomes greater than the sum of the parts; the team becomes greater than the sum of the talent of the individual players. We achieve far more than we ever thought possible.

When we achieve that intense level of teamwork, we stun our adversaries. We amaze our fans. We even amaze ourselves.

I've been coaching for more than 30 years, and if there's one thing I've learned in all that time, it's that coaching is not primarily about X's and O's. Coaching is a "people business." And my biggest "people challenge" is to get my players to become outstanding teammates to each other.

Every Sunday before each game, I've been telling my players, "Go out there and be a great teammate." But I never really defined for them what that means.

Then I read *How to Be the Ultimate Teammate* by Pat Williams. This book defines the 15 dimensions of an Ultimate Teammate. With dozens of stories and an engaging, conversational style, Pat shows each of us how to become the best teammate anybody ever had.

I am going to use this book with my team, because I'm working to develop a roster of Ultimate Teammates. If all my players are Ultimate Teammates, we will be in the best position to compete for a championship on a yearly basis.

If you love team sports, if you love your team and your players, you're going to love this book.

Marc Trestman
Head Coach, Chicago Bears
Author, *Perseverance: Life Lessons on Leadership and Teamwork*

CONTENTS

INTRODUCTION
The Best Teammate Anybody Has Ever Had

"You shouldn't just work on your jump shot. You should work on being a better person, a better teammate, and a better friend."

—Coach Sue Wicks

In the 2004 NBA Draft, the Orlando Magic took center Dwight Howard of Southwest Atlanta Christian Academy with our first pick. Then, we made a trade to acquire another first-round pick later in the draft, and we selected a six-foot point guard from Saint Joseph's University in Philadelphia. His name: Jameer Nelson. That was a decade ago, and Jameer has been our point guard ever since.

When Jameer Nelson played college basketball at St. Joe's, he often made this statement: "My only goal in basketball is to be the best teammate anybody has ever had." I have quoted Jameer's words many times in my speaking, and I have seen the impact those words have on people in the sports world—not only among coaches and athletes, but among people in the business world and in the church world. Wherever people come together in a team or organization to achieve great things, this should be everyone's goal: to be the best teammate anybody has ever had—to be, in short, the Ultimate Teammate.

When I first heard Jameer make that statement, I thought, *Those words need to be thumb-tacked to the wall of every locker room, every office, every business cubicle in America. Those words need to be pinned up in every military barracks, on every church bulletin board, in every family's kitchen.*

We should all commit to the goal of being the Ultimate Teammate, the best teammate anybody has ever had. If all of us would put that principle into practice, we would transform our teams, organizations, churches, families, communities, and nation. If we, as citizens, would practice that principle and work together as Ultimate Teammates, reaching across divisions of race, culture, religion, and politics, we could transform the world and eliminate most of the ills and injustices of our age.

Over the past few decades, I have received many requests to speak to sports teams at every level, from high school to college to professional teams. Having written a number of books on teamwork, I'm often asked to speak on the subject of building great teams.

On one occasion, when I was about to give a talk on teamwork, Jameer Nelson's words sprang to mind. The thought hit me: *You can't build a great team without great teammates*. I had always looked at teamwork from the coach's point of view, from the perspective of team leadership. In that moment, I saw the whole issue of teamwork from a totally different perspective: the player's perspective.

I asked myself: What are the ingredients that make up the Ultimate Teammate? What are the qualities that have to be present in my life in order for me to become the best teammate anybody has ever had?

In those moments, I felt inspired to write a totally new speech that I call "The Ultimate Teammate." I snatched up a pen and a yellow legal pad and began scribbling ideas as fast as they would come—and the ideas seemed to come out of nowhere. It was an amazing brainstorming session. It lasted about 15 minutes. When it was over, I looked at the pages I had just filled with notes. The ideas I had written down seemed amazingly complete and well-organized. I had just written a speech in 15 minutes.

I later realized that I had written that speech during an experience of heightened awareness known as being "in the zone." I can recall four other "in the zone" experiences I've had, all of them occurring in my early athletic career.

Once, during a high school basketball game, I entered that zone in which I drained every shot I put up from the outside; in fact, the moment the ball left my hands, I knew it would go in, and it did—seemingly in slow motion. And during a high school baseball game, I had an incredible "in the zone" experience in which I hit two home runs and a line-drive single because, when I was at bat, every pitch seemed to cross the plate in slow motion and I knew with absolute clarity whether or not to take a swing. I had another zone experience during my baseball career at Wake Forest University—I went four for five, including a home run on a fake bunt and swing. And in my first year in pro ball, 1962, I got four hits in one game—each time, I felt like I was hitting off a batting tee.

Many athletes know that strange and wonderful "in the zone" experience. Time seems to slow down. You feel you could count the stitches on the fastball as it goes over the plate. You feel physically, mentally, and spiritually elevated to a whole new level of performance. That's how I felt during the 15 minutes when I was writing that speech on my yellow legal pad. I was fully in the zone.

If I were to try to rewrite that speech from scratch right now, I couldn't do it. It was one of those in-the-moment experiences—15 minutes in which everything was clicking, and I was writing down thoughts as quickly as they came to me. It was a flash of inspiration that vanished as quickly as it came. Fortunately, I got it all written down.

I have given that speech scores and scores of times, and the response to that speech is always enthusiastic. And I have to give credit where credit is due. I have to give thanks to God for inspiring that speech and giving me the presence of mind to write it all down. And I have to give credit to Jameer Nelson, whose simple formulation sparked all the ideas that flowed through my mind and onto that yellow legal pad: "My only goal in basketball is to be the best teammate anybody has ever had." Those words may sound simple, but they encapsulate an insight for the ages.

And now, I have expanded that speech into the book you hold in your hands—*How to Be the Ultimate Teammate*. I have turned the 15 principles of that speech into 15 chapters. I believe you'll find each of those principles to be powerful, life-changing, yet simple to understand and apply to your everyday life. When you finish this book, you'll have all the tools you need to be the best teammate anybody ever had.

Imagine if you and all your teammates become Ultimate Teammates, the very best teammates anybody could ever want. Imagine an entire roster filled with Ultimate Teammates. It would be nothing less than the Ultimate Team, performing at an ultimate level, practicing the ultimate in teamwork. Such a team would be unstoppable.

But you can't have an Ultimate Team without Ultimate Teammates. And it all begins with you.

You've taken the first step by reading this far. Now turn the page. Just 15 more steps to go!

1

EMPOWER OTHERS

"Empower your teammates on and off the court. This is the sign of a true leader. Your title makes you the captain, but your teammates make you a leader."

The February 16, 2004 cover of *Sports Illustrated* featured Jameer Nelson in his red Saint Joseph's Hawks uniform with the headline, "Meet Jameer Nelson: The Little Man from the Little School That's Beating Everyone." The feature story tells how Jameer grew up in Chester, Pennsylvania, midway between Philadelphia and Wilmington, Delaware. He lettered in basketball at Chester High School, then played for St. Joseph's University in Philadelphia from 2000 to 2004. During his senior year, he led St. Joe's to a 27-0 regular-season record, and he won the 2004 Wooden Award, the 2004 Naismith Award, the 2004 Bob Cousy Award, the Rupp Trophy, the Oscar Robertson Trophy, and many other accolades.

Despite Jameer's many individual achievements, his most memorable and distinguishing qualities are those that set him apart as a teammate. His Saint Joseph's coach, Phil Martelli, said this about his star player near the end of Jameer's senior year: "Jameer is a unique, once-in-a-lifetime person, not just a basketball player. He is every bit as good a person as he is a basketball player. And I will miss him sitting around the office at ten o'clock in the morning, just laughing and talking, as much as I will miss him playing against St. Bonaventure or Temple or Xavier or whomever. He is that unique as an individual."[1]

Jameer was selected 20th in the 2004 NBA Draft by the Denver Nuggets, and the Nuggets traded him to the Magic for a 2005 first-round draft pick. He has played his entire NBA career in Orlando. Throughout his Magic career, he has been the same kind of caring, committed, competitive teammate that he was at St. Joe's. Five years into his career with the Magic, the sports website BleacherReport.com insightfully observed: "Since making it out of the crime infested Philadelphia suburb of Chester, Nelson has been a model teammate while in the NBA."

One of the most important ways that Jameer Nelson is a "model teammate" is by being an empowerer to his fellow players. His old coach at St. Joe's, Phil Martelli, told me a story that illustrates how Jameer always sought to empower his teammates.

"I allowed walk-ons to try out for our squad," Martelli told me. "At the beginning of the 2003–2004 season, two kids got to the final cuts. I told one of them he had made the team, then I called the other one into my office to tell him we didn't have a spot for him. His name was Andrew Koefer."

Andrew Koefer was a freshman from Central Catholic High School in Allentown, Pennsylvania. Meanwhile, Jameer Nelson was well on his way to becoming the consensus national Player of the Year, an All-American, and a first-round NBA draft pick. A lot of players at Jameer Nelson's level would have scarcely noticed a freshman player like Koefer. But what happened next is what makes Jameer Nelson such a great teammate. Martelli recalled:

> Koefer and I were sitting in my office and I was about to give him the consolation speech—"Well, you worked real hard and did your best,

but it just wasn't enough to get you on the team." Before I could say anything, my secretary knocked on my door and said, "Coach—Jameer is on the phone and he says he needs to talk to you." I figured I'd better speak to my All-American, so I picked up the phone.

Jameer said, "Coach, what are you doing right now?" I told him I was talking to Andrew Koefer. Jameer said, "Don't cut the kid from the team, Coach. He can help us. He's a good competitor." I said, "Jameer, does it mean that much to you?" He said, "Yes. This kid has a dream, and I am on this earth to help people's dreams come true."

That was good enough for me. I hung up the phone and instead of telling Andrew Koefer he was cut, I congratulated him for making the team. And that's the kind of teammate Jameer was to everyone at St. Joe's. He wasn't there just to play basketball and win games. He was there to help make his teammates' dreams come true.

In other words, Jameer was there to *empower* his teammates.

Great Teammates Are Great Empowerers

Empowerment means different things to different people. When I use the word *empowerment*, I'm talking about the act of motivating and encouraging others by cheering them on, praising them, boosting them, supporting them, and helping to make their dreams come true. An empowerer is someone who is always lifting others up and helping others believe in themselves. An empowerer is the head cheerleader on your team.

Writer Naomi Klein has often criticized the American athletic equipment company Nike, but she also observes that Nike has tapped into a universal human longing through its most famous advertising slogan. Klein writes, "We are looking to brands for poetry and for spirituality, because we're not getting those things from our communities or from each other. When Nike says, 'Just Do It,' that's a message of empowerment. Why aren't the rest of us speaking … in a voice of inspiration?"[2]

The word *empower* means exactly what it says: when you give people a word of encouragement and affirmation, you actually inspire and endow them with *power*, the motivation and emotional energy to achieve great things.

Great teammates are great empowerers. They lift their fellow players with messages of empowerment, enabling their entire team to magnify the effectiveness of their talent, skill, coaching, and strategy. Empowerment gives your team an added edge—and maybe just the edge you need to pull out a win in a clutch situation. Even simple messages like "Good job!" and "'Attaboy!" and simple acts like giving credit where credit is due can lift a team to unimagined heights of confidence and achievement.

Swen Nater is a Dutch-born basketball center who played for Coach John Wooden at UCLA, and went on to a 12-year career in pro basketball. He once told me a story about the summer between his junior and senior years playing for Coach Wooden. Legendary Lakers center Wilt Chamberlain had agreed to work out with Swen at UCLA's Pauley Pavilion and give him a few pointers. Wilt went straight from the Santa Monica beach to the campus—then realized he'd forgotten to bring his basketball shoes. So Wilt asked Swen, "You want to come with me while I pick up my shoes?"

Swen was thrilled to ride with Wilt in his big red El Dorado convertible. Wilt invited Swen into his house and showed him his huge walk-in closet. Swen told me that Wilt's closet was twice as big as Swen's entire dorm room. Wilt and Swen wore the same size shoe, so the Lakers star gave Swen two pairs of Converse shoes.

Returning to campus, Swen and Wilt asked a couple of students to join them in a half-court game, 2-on-2. Wilt showed Swen some moves he'd never seen before. A few times, Swen went up for a rebound—then found himself dazed and lying on the hardwood, wondering what hit him. After a few pickup games, Swen was feeling beat-up and humiliated—even though he knew he was competing against one of the greatest players in NBA history.

But then Wilt said something to Swen that completely changed his mood: "I like the way you rebound," Wilt said. "You could have a career in the NBA if you want to."

What a message of empowerment! If Wilt said it, Swen believed it. Those words motivated Swen throughout his college career and on into his long career in professional basketball. Players who empower their fellow players with messages of respect and encouragement have an impact far beyond what they imagine.

Nine Principles of Empowerment

As author Jim Stovall so wisely said; "You need to be aware of what others are doing, applaud their efforts, acknowledge their successes, and encourage them in their pursuits. When we all help one another, everybody wins."[3] Following are some principles of empowerment to help you become the Ultimate Empowering Teammate on your team or in your organization.

Be selfless when you empower your teammates.

Empowerment is not a quid pro quo. It's not a matter of you empower me and I'll empower you. We should empower others without expecting anything in return.

The late UCLA basketball coach John Wooden put it this way: "There is always great joy in learning that something you've said or done has been meaningful to another, especially when you do it without any thought of receiving anything in return. Your gift doesn't even have to be material. Helping others in any way—with a smile, a nod, or a pat on the back—warms the heart."[4]

People need empowerment more in times of failure than in times of success.

People crave an affirming word *especially* after they've made a mistake or suffered a setback. It's one thing to say "Good job!" when someone does something well—and that kind of empowerment is important. But in times of failure, players need a different kind of empowerment. Instead of saying "Good job," you might say, "Don't let it get you down. Don't be too hard on yourself. You'll succeed next time. You're going to do just fine. I foresee a great future for you." Let your teammates know that, even when they fail, you're still pulling for them and cheering them on.

When Dwight Howard played center for the Orlando Magic, he and Stan Van Gundy (the Magic's head coach from 2007 to 2012) sometimes struggled with each other's personalities. Dwight sometimes felt he didn't get the affirmation he needed from Coach Van Gundy. So Dwight and Stan met together to clear the air.

After the meeting, Dwight told reporters: "Players sometimes are like little puppies. We want to be patted on the head even if we make a mistake."

Coach Van Gundy also talked to reporters about that meeting. "I asked [Dwight] what he thought was going on." He added that Dwight told him there were problems on the team because of the pressure of expectations and, as Stan put it, "my negativity."

According to the *Orlando Sentinel*, after the "summit" between Dwight Howard and Coach Van Gundy, "players noticed the difference in Van Gundy's behavior on the bench." Power forward Rashard Lewis said, "Stan was great. He was coaching instead of bashing us. He'd bash us two minutes into a time-out and then coach us the rest of the way … . He doesn't need to be a nice man for us to play hard."[5]

It's true. A little bit of empowerment goes a long way. And when Van Gundy focused more on empowerment, the Magic went on a winning streak.

Gary Steele played tight end for Army's football team in the 1960s (he also broke the color barrier, becoming the first African-American to play football for Army). Steele recalled: "In 1966, we played a game at Notre Dame. We played well, but lost a tough one. After the game, I was walking up the tunnel to our locker when I felt this big arm wrap around my shoulder pads. Then I heard a deep voice in my ear, 'You played a really good game today.' I looked over and it was Alan Page, the great Notre Dame star. Over forty years later, I still remember every detail of that experience." A brief word of encouragement and empowerment can take a lot of the sting out of defeat.

When you boost a teammate's confidence, you almost always boost his performance.

A well-chosen word of encouragement can summon incredible effort, even from a mediocre performer.

The late Major League Baseball pitcher and manager Clyde King recalled:

> People always ask me what made Roy Campanella such a great catcher. To me, what made him a great catcher was that he could make you think you were Walter Johnson or Sandy Koufax or Bob Gibson or any of the other great pitchers. For someone like me, who wasn't a top pitcher at all, Campy did wonders for my psyche.
>
> He would come out to the mound and when he knew that I couldn't get someone out he'd improvise, as he did with our famous quick-pitch on Willie Mays. He would say things like, "Hey, we've got two strikes on this guy, and I've seen you make great two-strike pitches. Let's see you make one here."
>
> Campy was the ultimate confidence-builder. He could make you think you could get anybody out.

When a teammate thinks he can do the "impossible," he often does.

Compliment strong effort and good performance.

Don't go overboard. Don't lavish empty praise. But when your teammates do well, let them know.

Gary Knafelc, who played tight end for the Green Bay Packers under Coach Vince Lombardi, recalls that one day after a training camp practice on the campus of St. Norbert University, he and quarterback Bart Starr were heading back to their room. Knafelc had the feeling they were being followed, so he looked back and sure enough, there was Coach Lombardi, striding up behind them and gaining on them. Knafelc was terrified of Lombardi, and he said to Starr, "He's behind us!"

Knafelc and Starr walked faster and crossed the street, but Coach Lombardi still gained on them. Knafelc felt panicky and thought, *Oh, no. Coach is trying to catch up to me so he can tell me he's cutting me from the team!* Finally, Lombardi pulled up alongside them and said to Knafelc, "You had some good blocks today." Then he strode on by.

A compliment from Coach Lombardi was a rare treat—and the fact that his compliments were so carefully chosen made them especially valuable. Knafelc later recalled, "That one [compliment] carried me through the entire season."

Coach Tom Coughlin, former head coach of the New York Giants, put it this way: "There is no better reinforcement than a compliment. Just a few words of praise—'Nice job, way to go'—coming from a person you respect can carry tremendous weight. It can make you want to bust through a wall if that's what it takes to earn that praise."[6]

If you want to empower your teammates, acknowledge them by name.

We feel affirmed and inspired when someone we respect calls us by name.

Tito Francona was a Major League outfielder and first baseman who played for a number of teams (notably the Baltimore Orioles, Cleveland Indians, and St. Louis Cardinals) from 1956 to 1970. At the beginning of his Major League career, Francona experienced an empowering moment of recognition—not from a teammate but from an opponent. He recalled:

> I remember when I first come up with Baltimore, first game in the big leagues, and you know I'm nervous. I got butterflies and all, so I get to the ballpark around six a.m. We're playing the Red Sox and I'm walking along the tunnel and I see this big number nine coming toward me—it's Ted Williams. And he says, "Hey, you're Tito Francona." And I'm thinking, How do *you* know who I am? And he tells me he was once teammates with my roommate Harry Dorish, and Harry told him to look out for me. And Ted was great, gave me advice on hitting and everything, told me not to use such a heavy bat when the weather got warm.[7]

It means a lot to us when people acknowledge us by name. Whenever you greet a teammate, hand out a compliment, or empower your teammate in any way, call your teammate by name. You'll add a little oomph to your empowerment.

Give your teammates your time and attention.

When you pay attention to your fellow players—to their interests, hopes, wants, and needs—you empower them to achieve great things.

In 1998, Sage Steele (who, incidentally, is the daughter of Gary Steele, mentioned earlier) was a local TV news journalist working at an ABC affiliate in Tampa, Florida. Along with her then-fiancé (now husband), she boarded a flight for a visit to her parents' home in Connecticut. As they moved down the aisle, Sage noticed one of their fellow passengers—Robin Roberts, then an anchor of ESPN *SportsCenter*, and now a *Good Morning America* co-host. Sage turned to her fiancé and whispered, "Look! It's Robin Roberts! She's my hero!"

Sage and her fiancé continued down the aisle and took their seats. Through most of the flight, she wondered, *Should I approach Robin Roberts? Should I give her my card and ask her to look at one of my tapes? Maybe she'd give me some constructive criticism.* She had a VHS demo video tape she had brought to show her parents. Should she give the tape to Roberts?

She finally made up her mind, got out of her seat, went forward, and woke Roberts from a nap. The ESPN anchor was pleasant and gracious. When Sage gave her the video tape, Roberts promised to view it. Later, after the plane landed, Roberts actually waited for Sage to get off the plane and walked with her to the baggage claim area, giving her encouragement and promising to get back to her. Two weeks later, Roberts wrote to Sage, sending her a note of encouragement, praise, and constructive pointers. Sage was thrilled.

More than a decade later, after Sage herself had become an ESPN *SportsCenter* anchor, she attended the National Association of Black Journalists Convention. She was on a panel at a breakfast attended by 500 people—and she shared the panel with her hero, Robin Roberts. During the panel discussion, Roberts turned to Sage, her voice choking with emotion, and said, "Sage, keep it up. I can't believe I'm getting choked up right now, but when I watch you every morning, I see so much of me in you. You are amazing. You're setting a great example for young women everywhere, especially young black women who don't know if there's a chance of getting into this business. You're fabulous. I'm so proud of you."

Sage was moved and empowered by Robin Roberts' words. She later recalled, "I just couldn't believe it! … This is the woman I strive to be like … It just floored me."[8]

When you give time and attention to your teammates, when you take a genuine personal interest in other people and their hopes and dreams, you empower them in a big way.

Don't give up—keep empowering.

Even when your teammate seems unresponsive or unappreciative of your encouragement and empowerment, you may still be getting through.

On May 25, 1965, a heavyweight championship fight was held in the tiny town of Lewiston, Maine. The combatants: Muhammad Ali and Sonny Liston. Ali had wrested the title from Liston the previous year in a shocking upset. Now they were meeting for a rematch. Because Ali was a recent convert to the Nation of Islam, which was undergoing factional disputes following the assassination of Malcolm X, there were rumors of potential gun violence at the fight. Fewer than 2,500 fans attended the fight at St. Dominic's Hall in Lewiston.

Less than two minutes into the first round, Ali delivered a straight right to Liston's chin, felling the former champ. Liston lay writhing on the canvas while Ali stood over him, taunting. Referee Jersey Joe Walcott struggled to shove Muhammad Ali back to a neutral corner, losing track of the count. Liston finally got back on his feet, but an official timekeeper shouted to Walcott that Liston had been down for the 10-count. Walcott raised Muhammad Ali's arm and declared him the winner.

To the fans in the arena, that straight right from Ali's glove didn't look like a knockout blow. The crowd shouted, "Fake! Fake!" To this day, sports historians question whether the flight was fixed. But one thing is certain: Sonny Liston was humiliated.

One of the spectators in the arena that night was former heavyweight champion Floyd Patterson, who had lost his title to Sonny Liston in 1962. In fact, Patterson had lost his title under similar circumstances, suffering a first-round knockout that was widely questioned by fans and sportswriters. So Patterson knew what it felt like to be accused of taking a dive.

After the fight, Patterson went to Liston's dressing room to console him. Patterson later recalled:

> [Liston] was all by himself [in the dressing room]. I said to him, "I know how you feel. I've experienced this myself." And [Liston] didn't say one word. He didn't say anything. He just kept looking and looking, [and] he had that mean look on his face. I don't think he knew he had the mean look. But I kept on talking anyway. And finally I said [to myself] I don't think I'm reaching him. So I said, "Okay, I'll see you later." So I went to walk out the door and before I could get out the door, he ran up and put his arms on my shoulder and I turned around, and he said, "Thanks." I knew then that I'd reached him.[9]

Don't stop trying to empower your teammates, even when they have "that mean look," even when they seem unresponsive. Keep talking, keep empowering. They'll hear you, and they'll come around.

Make empowerment vivid and memorable.

Find ways to make your acts of empowerment tangible and unforgettable. Send handwritten cards and notes. Give a plaque with a motivational or inspirational quote. Or take a cue from a legendary Major League Baseball pitcher.

Orel Hershiser holds the record for most consecutive scoreless innings pitched—59 consecutive innings without giving up a run, from August 30, 1988, to September 28, 1988. That year, he won the Cy Young Award and was voted World Series MVP. He played 18 seasons in the majors, including 13 with the Los Angeles Dodgers.

After the Dodgers spring training camp in 1992, Hershiser learned that a young pitcher on the team was being sent back to the minors. So Hershiser inscribed a baseball and slipped it into the young pitcher's bag. Later, when the rookie found the ball in his bag, he read: "From one big leaguer to another. See you back here soon. Orel Hershiser."

Orel's inscription was empowering—and prophetic. That rooky pitcher's name was Pedro Martinez, and he did in fact go on to a highly successful career in the big leagues.[10] Sometimes words of empowerment are not enough. Find something tangible, something meaningful that you can give a teammate—a symbol of empowerment that your teammate can hold, display, and look at again and again.

You're never too old to give or receive a word of empowerment.

Once, when I was in my late 50s, I was catching in a Phillies fantasy game. Ed Liberatore, the longtime Dodgers scout, was at the game. Afterward, he came up to me and said, "You looked terrific out there. Good hands. You blocked well. I'd put you down as a prospect."

Ed was kidding, of course, but his compliments on my playing that day were real. He made me feel like a million bucks!

So if you want to become the Ultimate Teammate, if you have made it your goal to be the best teammate anybody has ever had, then here's the place to start: *become an empowerer*. Lift the performance of your team by lifting the spirits and confidence of your teammates. You'll be amazed at how the very act of empowering others injects a shot of motivation and empowerment into your own soul.

2

"Hard work spotlights the character of people: some turn up their sleeves, some turn up their noses, and some don't turn up at all."

—Outfielder Sam Ewing

Jameer Nelson has gone out of his way to be an outstanding teammate by working hard and going the extra mile. Every year during the off-season, he hosts a training session in Philadelphia for his Magic teammates—something I've never seen any other NBA player do.

Every August, Jameer brings his teammates into Philadelphia for a three-day session of teaching, financial counseling, and basketball workouts. They also attend a Phillies game and take a relaxing trip to Atlantic City. Jameer plans and hosts the entire event as a way of caring for his teammates and helping to prepare them for the upcoming season. There are no coaches at this event, just players—and that helps to make it a time a bonding among teammates.

Players arrive on Sunday, gather at Summit Sports in Bryn Mawr for a morning workout (weights, running, yoga, and even some boxing), move to Haverford College for an afternoon of basketball (sometimes joined by players from the 76ers, Villanova, or St. Joe's), then have a team dinner together in the evening.

In all my years of pro basketball, I've never seen anything like it.

The message Jameer sends to his teammates is profound: We don't have to limit ourselves to the "official" training and workout schedule. Be willing to give your teammates more work, more effort, more hustle than is expected of you. Let's give each other all the effort we've got—then let's see where it takes us.

To be the best teammate anybody has ever had, you have to give your teammates your maximum effort. You've got to work hard and go above and beyond the call of duty.

Hustle a Little More

Peanuts Riley was my coach in a semi-pro baseball league when I was in high school. Peanuts had been a Minor League infielder in the Phillies system, and he loved baseball and knew the game inside-out. He always took an interest in those who loved the game as much as he did. He knew I was passionate about baseball.

When I went away to college, Peanuts wrote a note of encouragement to me. I kept that note folded up in my wallet for years. His advice left a huge impression on me: "Hustle a little more every day. Don't ever lose your confidence. Remember, the other fellows put their uniforms on the same way you do. Never stop swinging, and you'll be rough on all of them." In other words, *work hard* if you want to be a great teammate.

Wade Boggs is a former third baseman who spent his 18-year baseball career playing for the Red Sox, Yankees, and Devil Rays. During an interview he gave when he was inducted into the Baseball Hall of Fame, Boggs said, "I played the game one way. I gave it everything I had. It doesn't take any ability to hustle … When I retired in 1999, I grounded out to second and gave it everything I had running down to first base in my last at-bat. I always felt if I disrespected the game by not hustling and giving everything

I had, it's cheating the fans … You're cheating your teammates and disrespecting the name that's on the front of your jersey … Nowadays it's fashionable not to hustle. I just don't understand it."[11]

Tom Smith, a former athletic trainer for the Orlando Magic, told me a story over lunch one day that sheds light on the work ethic of the great L.A. Lakers shooting guard Kobe Bryant:

> One morning in mid-summer, I came to work at the Magic facility and looked in the weight room. Over in the corner I saw an athlete working out—and I did a double-take when I realized it was Kobe Bryant. I thought, *Wow! What's Kobe doing in our facility at this time of year?* So I went up to him and said, "Kobe, what brings you here in the off-season?"
>
> He said that he was in Orlando with his family out for a week-long vacation at Disney World. I asked him about his workout schedule. He explained that he got up at five in the morning, came to our facility at six, and worked out hard until nine. Then he showered, drove 30 miles back to the hotel, picked up his family, and got to Disney World by 11. He kept up that schedule every day, Monday through Friday, throughout his vacation. If anyone wants to know why Kobe Bryant is one of the best players in the game today, there it is. The man has a tough-minded work ethic all year round.

In short, Kobe hustles. That's the kind of hustle Coach John Wooden spoke of when he said, "Give me 100 percent. You can't make up for a poor effort today by giving 110 percent tomorrow. You don't have 110 percent. You only have 100 percent, and that's what I want from you right now."[12]

Work Creates Value

A number of years ago, I had lunch with a prominent business leader. During our visit, he told me a story about his 10-year-old son, Alan. He said that while he was tucking his son into bed the previous night, the boy said, "Dad, when you die, will I get half your money?"

The man was surprised. "Why would you ask that, Alan?"

"Well, Dad," the boy replied, "you are getting kind of old. I just wanted to know."

"Alan, rather than me giving you half of my money when I die, wouldn't you rather go out into the world and earn your money through hard work? Wouldn't that give you a greater sense of accomplishment?"

Alan thought for a moment, then said, "Actually, Dad, I'd rather you just give me the money."

That's an honest expression of human nature. We're lazy, we want what we want, and we'd rather not have to work hard for it. Hard work goes against our grain as human beings. We want "success," and we want lots of "stuff," and we don't want to earn it—we want it handed to us. We're a lazy, greedy species.

Achievers are people who conquer their natural human tendency to be undisciplined and unmotivated, so that they can accomplish great things through maximum effort. Achievers understand that *work creates value*. The more effectively and productively you work, the more valuable you are to the team and to your teammates.

Bill Russell, the great Boston Celtics center who played for Coach Red Auerbach from 1956 to 1969, recalled, "Red appreciated my work ethic, which came from my father. When I was about six, my dad sat me down and told me, 'Son, I don't know what you'll be when you grow up, but here's what I want you to think about. When you take a job, if they pay you two dollars a day, give them three dollars worth of work. The reason is, if they're paying you two and you're giving them three, you're more valuable to them than they are to you.'"[13]

That's great advice. Hard work produces effective results that make you a valued and valuable member of the team. A teammate who won't work hard contributes nothing of value to the team and to his teammates. When he's gone, he won't be missed.

Sid Luckman quarterbacked the Chicago Bears for 12 seasons, from 1939 to 1950, leading the Bears to four NFL championships. He was considered the greatest long-range passer of his era. Sportswriters and coaches of his time did not consider Luckman to have great natural talent as a quarterback. He had the wrong physique, and he lacked the speed and agility that marks most great quarterbacks. But Sid Luckman had a quality that set him apart from other quarterbacks of his era: he was committed to working harder than anyone else on the field.

George Halas, the owner and coach of the Bears, said this of his star quarterback: "Sid made himself a great quarterback. No one else did it for him. He worked hard, stayed up nights studying and really learned the T-formation. Sid wasn't built for quarterback. He was stocky, not fast, and not a great passer in the old tradition. But he was smart and he was dedicated."[14]

Internet entrepreneur Sam Parker is the author of a motivational book called *212: The Extra Degree*. The book opens with these words: "At 211 degrees, water is hot. At 212 degrees, it boils. And with boiling water, comes steam. And with steam, you can power a train."[15] The message is clear: An extra degree of effort makes all the difference in the world.

One achiever who has bought into the 212-degree work ethic is New Orleans Saints quarterback Drew Brees. After moving to New Orleans in 2006 to play for the Saints, Brees gave the team's head coach, Sean Payton, a copy of *212: The Extra Degree* with a hand-written inscription: "I want to win a championship for you."

Payton said that the book, with that inscription, reenergized him as a coach, because it was clear to him that Drew Brees is dedicated to delivering that one extra degree of effort. "Everything about Drew's preparation," Coach Payton said, "is about that extra degree."

Payton told a story that illustrates the extra degree of effort Drew Brees gives to the game. "During the bye week," Payton said, "players are getting out of here. I was leaving the building on Sunday, and out on the field I see this guy in shorts with a ball. It's Brees out there by himself, Sunday, 1:30. And I say, 'What are you doing?' He says, 'I'm just trying to stay in my routine, simulate a game, so my body is still in condition.'"[16]

How many players in any sport would spend their bye week playing a mock game just to maintain their readiness for next week's game? That's a competitor who is giving 212 degrees of effort. He is never content with 211 degrees. As one of Brees's teammates, linebacker Scott Fujita, observed: "Drew just outworks everybody."[17]

Hard Work Makes It Look Easy

Sports broadcaster Red Barber was a play-by-play commentator for the Cincinnati Reds from 1934 to 1938, the Brooklyn Dodgers from 1939 to 1953, and the New York Yankees from 1954 to 1966. He was fascinated by the interaction of natural talent and disciplined effort to produce an outstanding athletic performance. His curiosity led him to investigate athletic performances beyond the field of baseball—including the performances of dancer and movie star Fred Astaire.

With astonishing athleticism and an air of nonchalance, Fred Astaire could dance on tabletops, walk up walls, and float around the dance floor as if the law of gravity had been repealed. Astaire made it look effortless. So when Red Barber had the opportunity to interview Astaire, he asked the star of *Top Hat* and *Swing Time* if his dancing ability came naturally to him.

Barber recalled: "I was interested … to find out the correlation between his dancing and athletic ability. And to my surprise he said, 'Well, I wouldn't say that dancing comes so easily to me. I work at it. I practice hour after hour,' and suddenly you see a man who does something so effortlessly—seemingly effortlessly—and you find out that each of us who are genuine professionals pays a price."[18]

The price we pay for making it look easy is hours and hours of hard work. The more effort we put into our performance, the more effortless it appears. And when people watch us perform, they say, "What magnificent talent!" Let them think your performance comes easily to you. But you and I know that the secret to your "talent" is hard work.

Heisman-winning quarterback Tim Tebow, who has played for the Broncos and Jets in the NFL, says he has lived by one maxim since he was six years old: "Hard work beats talent when talent doesn't work hard." Tebow adds, "Every day, I'm trying to go out there and outwork everybody else. It doesn't matter if you're more talented and more blessed than me, I'm going to outwork you every day of the week."[19]

Hard work is not merely a matter of putting in time. It's what you do with your time that counts. Many of us put in long hours while accomplishing little. Success guru Brian Tracy, in his book *Million Dollar Habits*, explains why putting in long hours alone does not equal working effectively and productively:

> One of the most important habits you can develop ... is the habit of working all the time you work. According to Robert Half International, the average employee works only 50 percent of the time. The other 50 percent of working time is largely wasted. It is spent in idle chitchat and conversation with co-workers, late arrivals, extended coffee breaks and lunches, and early departures. It is dribbled away making private phone calls, reading the newspaper, taking care of personal business, and surfing the Internet ... .
>
> Resolve to work all the time you work. Start a little earlier, and when you get in, go to work immediately ... . Keep repeating to yourself the mantra, "Back to work! Back to work! Back to work!" Tell your co-workers that you can socialize with them after work, if you have the time. And then get back to work.[20]

Don't be a clock-watcher. When you are working, give it your maximum effort. As former White Sox outfielder Sam Ewing once said: "It's not the hours you put in your work that counts. It's the work you put in your hours."

Effort Inspires *More* Effort

Former offensive lineman Jerry Kramer played his entire eleven-year NFL career with the Green Bay Packers, much of it under legendary head coach Vince Lombardi. Kramer recalled that Coach Lombardi taught his players an all-important principle of hard work. Kramer quotes Lombardi as saying, "The harder you work, the harder it is to surrender ... . If you quit now, during these workouts, you'll quit in the middle of the season, during a game. Once you learn to quit, it becomes a habit. We don't want anyone here who'll quit. We want 100 percent out of every individual, and if you don't want to give it, get out. Just get up and get out, right now."[21]

One of the reasons a team needs players who work hard is that effort inspires more effort. One hard-working player can elevate the total effort of the entire team. Former Angels right fielder Tim Salmon explained it this way: "Champions are the guys that work hard, don't give up, believe in themselves, and try to make other people around them better."[22] Champions make their teammates better by the example they set through their own indomitable work ethic.

Legendary Alabama head football coach Bear Bryant taught his players that the best way to get more effort out of your teammates is by demanding more effort from yourself. "Work hard," he said. "There is no substitute for hard work. None. If you work hard, the folks around you are going to work harder."[23]

Coach Bryant reasoned that if a hard-working player inspires greater effort from his teammates, then the converse of that principle must also be true: lazy players infect their teammates with an attitude of laziness. That's why Coach Bryant also said, "Don't tolerate lazy people. They are losers. People who come to work and watch clocks and pass off responsibilities will only drag you and your organization down …. If you have lazy people, get rid of them. Remember, it is easy to develop the bad habits of lazy people."[24]

The iron-man work ethic of Coach Bryant went back to his early days as a young football coach at Kentucky. "I was determined I was going to outwork everybody," he later recalled, "and I worked day and night … . If [my assistant] coaches were due at 5:30, I got there at five."[25]

A player who works hard is always ready to get in the game and help his teammates achieve their goals. Retired NBA coach Hubie Brown tells about a backup center who made an impression on Brown when he was an assistant coach with the Milwaukee Bucks in the early 1970s. The backup center was 6'10" Dick Cunningham, but Hubie Brown called him "The Mixer." Cunningham was a backup for star center Kareem Abdul-Jabbar, the greatest player of his era—so The Mixer saw very little playing time in those years, usually no more than a minute or so per game.

Why was Coach Brown so impressed with his backup center? Because Dick Cunningham worked incredibly hard. After every practice, when the rest of the team headed for the showers, Dick "The Mixer" Cunningham would run up and down the stairs, over and over, building his endurance and stamina. One day, Hubie Brown asked, "Mixer, why do you run the stairs every day when you know you're not going to play?"

Cunningham replied, "Coach, one day Kareem's going down, and I gotta be ready."[26]

I don't know why Hubie Brown called Dick Cunningham "The Mixer," but I do know this: if you want to be the best teammate anybody has ever had, you need to follow the example of The Mixer. You've got to work hard every day, put out 212 degrees of effort, and make sure you're ready to play when your team needs you. As Magic Johnson once said, "Ask not what your teammates can do for you. Ask what you can do for your teammates."

To be the Ultimate Teammate, put forth your ultimate effort every day.

3 MAINTAIN A CONSISTENT POSITIVE ATTITUDE

"Enthusiasm is contagious. It's difficult to remain neutral or indifferent in the presence of a positive thinker."

—Speaker Denis Waitley

Graeme Pitman/iStock/Thinkstock

Pat Carroll was one of Jameer Nelson's teammates at St. Joe's. When I asked Pat what Jameer's most impressive quality was as a teammate, he said it was Jameer's positive attitude. "Jameer was always about uplifting his teammates," Pat told me, "particularly after a tough loss. When things were going badly, he would step up and bring the team together. He'd go around the locker room and say, 'It's all right. We'll be back again.' I never saw Jameer in a bad mood. His optimism and enthusiasm always brought out the best in each of us."

Many players who excel in high school and college sports have a hard time maintaining a positive attitude when they reach the pros. The player who once basked in the glow of hero worship from the hometown crowd often finds it difficult to make the transition to being a rookie, a back-bencher, in the major leagues. He's hungry for attention and playing time, and he grows restless and dissatisfied in his new role. He becomes (in baseball parlance) a "clubhouse lawyer."

Joe Garagiola, the longtime baseball catcher and *Today Show* co-host, once defined a "clubhouse lawyer" as "a .210 hitter who isn't playing. He gripes about everything. His locker is too near the dryer. His shoes aren't ever shined right. His undershirt isn't dry. His bats don't have the good knots in them that the stars' bats have. He's not playing because his manager is dumb. When he does play he says, 'Well what do you expect? I ain't played in two weeks.' And he's a perpetual second guesser."[27] In short, he's a player who spreads negativity, pessimism, and disharmony wherever he goes.

Jameer Nelson is no "clubhouse lawyer." Arriving in Orlando, Jameer exhibited the same positive spirit he had always demonstrated at St. Joe's in Philadelphia. Despite all the accolades he had received, including the cover of *Sports Illustrated*, Jameer was content to be patient and positive as he warmed the bench, awaiting his time to shine.

During his rookie season, a reporter asked him why he maintained such an optimistic outlook when he was no longer a starter, as he had been in college. Jameer replied, "Somebody has to come off the bench, somebody has to play a role and I'm happy with my role … . I know where I am in my career now. I couldn't ask for a better situation. It's a perfect opportunity for me."[28]

If you want to be the best teammate anybody has ever had, then make it your goal to always exemplify optimism, enthusiasm, and a positive mental attitude.

The Four Ingredients of a Positive Attitude

Every airplane has an instrument on the cockpit panel called an "attitude indicator." This indicator shows the pilot the aircraft's orientation with respect to the horizon. Even if the pilot is unable to see the horizon due to rain, fog, or darkness, the attitude indicator tells the pilot whether the airplane's nose is pitched upward or downward, and whether the plane is flying level or banked to the right or left. The plane's attitude determines whether it climbs, descends, or turns.

In much the same way, your attitude determines your altitude. A positive attitude can send you higher and empower you to achieve greater heights than you ever imagined. A negative attitude can send you plummeting into depression. Whether your attitude is positive or negative, it tends to be self-reinforcing and self-perpetuating. Optimism magnifies all the positive circumstances of your life; pessimism can send you into a death-spiral of defeat and despair. So it's important to always monitor your attitude and keep it in the positive range.

As Wade Boggs put it in his induction speech at the Baseball Hall of Fame: "Our lives are not determined by what happens to us, but how we react to what happens, not by what life brings us, but the attitude that we bring to life. A positive attitude causes a chain reaction of positive thoughts, events and outcomes. It is a catalyst and it sparks extraordinary results."[29]

In my years of study of successful lives and great teammates, I have identified four ingredients that, in my view, make up a positive attitude:

Ingredient 1: An Open Mind

"If you don't expect the unexpected," said theologian Jürgen Moltmann, "you will never find it." An optimist expects the unexpected and embraces it with enthusiasm when it comes. A pessimist resents the unexpected as an unwelcome intrusion. Optimists are always open to new experiences, new ideas, new challenges, new adventures, and new ways of thinking. To be a great teammate, keep an open mind.

Ingredient 2: Confidence

Auto-maker Henry Ford once said: "Whether you think you can or think you can't—you're right."[30] In order to achieve our team goals, every player must believe in the team's success-ability. Confidence is contagious—it spread from player to player, lifting the hopes and dreams of the entire team. As Lebron James once said: "Your teammates give you the confidence. They give me the confidence all year, all postseason." When every player has confidence in his own ability and that of his teammates, the entire team becomes motivated to achieve great things.

Ingredient 3: Self-Reliance

The world doesn't owe us honors and awards. Achievements and success must be earned. Success is the result of planning, preparation, hard work, and perseverance. The late Robert L. Baseman, who had a successful three-decade career as an executive with *Enclopaedia Britannica*, once wrote:

> If you have the right attitude, you're more likely to see opportunities. I have a pin that I wear on my lapel every day. I give these pins to my people and to anyone I meet who wants one. It says one word—ATTITUDE.

That one word is the key to success in any field. And it's because you can control it. You can't control the weather, or your kids, or the economy, but you can control your attitude. You know, life doesn't owe you anything. It's what you make it.

You can decide to be successful or be a failure ... . You're the only one who's got the power to improve your attitude.[31]

Everyone deals with obstacles, setbacks, and problems. It does us no good to wallow in bitterness or self-pity. We have to choose a self-reliant attitude that says, "It doesn't matter if these problems are my fault or if someone else dumped them on me. It doesn't matter if my circumstances are fair or unfair. Only one thing matters: I have to make the decisions that will solve these problems and produce victory and success. I choose to have an optimistic, can-do, self-reliant attitude, for my own sake and the sake of my teammates."

Ingredient 4: Enthusiasm

The word *enthusiasm* comes from the Greek word *entheos*, meaning "inspired by God" or "filled with a divine spirit." All the successful people I have ever known are people with an inspired, excited, eager attitude. They love what they do and do what they love. What's more, they continually fire up the people around them with emotions of gusto, passion, and enthusiasm.

Coach Vince Lombardi used to tell his players: "If you aren't fired up with enthusiasm, you will be fired with enthusiasm." And Michael Jordan said: "I play to win, whether during practice or a real game. And I will not let anything get in the way of me and my competitive enthusiasm to win." So be inspired, be fired up with enthusiasm, and watch how your enthusiasm catches fire with the teammates around you.

Following are logical, cause-and-effect reasons why enthusiastic optimists are more likely to be winners than pessimists:
- Optimists love and enjoy what they do.
- Optimists have the self-confidence to set challenging goals.
- Optimists embrace change and welcome challenges.
- Optimists don't squander time and energy on negative thoughts.
- Optimists tend to be healthier than pessimists, because an optimistic mindset is beneficial to the heart, digestion, and immune system.
- Optimists persevere through adversity, because they believe problems and setbacks are temporary.
- Optimists are decisive; they believe their decisions will probably turn out right.
- Optimists have the self-confidence to work longer and try harder.

To become the best teammates anybody ever had, we must become communicators of enthusiasm and optimism. Where others see obstacles, we learn to see exciting challenges and opportunities.

The Power to Choose Your Attitude

In *The Winner's Edge*, speaker and business consultant Denis Waitley tells the story of Air Force Colonel George Hall, who was shot down over North Vietnam and spent more than five years in a POW camp. Even amid the fear and abuse of the North Vietnamese prison, Colonel Hall found a way to survive through his ability to choose his own attitude.

Barefoot, clad in black prison pajamas, and shut up in a tiny closet-sized cell, Hall was able to leave his prison through his imagination. He pictured himself out on the plush fairway of the Pebble Beach golf course on the northern California coast. In his mind's eye, he experienced every detail—the young caddy at his side, the sun warming his skin, the salty breeze wafting from the Pacific Ocean, the grassy fragrance of the freshly manicured fairway. In his mind, Colonel Hall studied each shot, measured each swing, sank each putt, all in his imagination. Day after day for more than five years, Colonel Hall played a perfect game of golf at Pebble Beach.

Why did Colonel George Hall play fantasy golf every day in his tiny prison cell? He did it because he knew he had a choice to make. He could surrender to despair—or he could set his mind free and enjoy a perfect round of golf on a perfectly golden day in California.

When Colonel Hall was finally released, he returned to the States, eager to finally play a *real* game of golf on a *real* golf course. Less than a month after his release, he took part in the New Orleans Open with pro golfer Orville Moody as his partner. In his first golf game since being shot down over North Vietnam, he shot an astonishing 76. When asked how he achieved such a phenomenal score, he chalked it up to all the imaginary golf games he had played. In his entire time as a POW, he explained, he had never putted a green in more than two strokes. His imaginary practice—and his positive attitude—had paid off.[32]

Another man who overcame the horrors of a hellish prison system was psychiatrist and Nazi death camp survivor Viktor Frankl. In his book *Man's Search for Meaning*, he wrote, "We who lived in concentration camps can remember the men who walked through the huts comforting others, giving away their last piece of bread. They may have been few in number, but they offer sufficient proof that everything can be taken from a man but one thing: the last of the human freedoms—to choose one's attitude in any given set of circumstances, to choose one's own way."[33]

Conditioned to Think Positively

"Champions aren't made in gyms," Muhammad Ali once said. "Champions are made from something they have deep inside them—a desire, a dream, a vision. They have to have last-minute stamina, they have to be a little faster. They have to have the skill and the will, but the will must be stronger than the skill."[34]

The Champ is talking about the power of a positive attitude, a positive will. I've seen the truth of those words proven out at every level of athletic competition, from my children's youth league soccer games to the NBA playoffs. Talent and skill are important factors, and an injury or bad officiating can hinder you. But those aren't the factors that determine championships. Again and again, championships are won by the team that demonstrates the most positive attitude, the strongest will to win, the greatest confidence. These are the qualities that compensate for deficiencies in talent and skill, and which enable teams to overcome bad breaks.

Dallas Cowboys head coach Jimmy Johnson gave a pep talk to his team just before the Cowboys' 1993 Super Bowl victory—and it was a speech entirely about a positive attitude. Johnson later told reporters:

> I told them that if I laid a two-by-four across the floor of the locker room, everybody there could walk across it and not fall, because our focus would be that we were going to walk that two-by-four. But if I put that same two-by-four ten stories high between two buildings, only a few would make it, because the focus would be on falling. Then I said, "Your focus right now has to be as if we're playing on the practice field in front of nobody ... . If you make it bigger than life, that will be a distraction." And that's the crux of this game.[35]

Johnson kept his team's focus on positive thoughts, on the will to win, not on the distractions surrounding the game. His players responded and went on to win the NFL championship.

As players, as teammates, we must condition ourselves to think positively. The average person sees problems and challenges as obstacles to be feared. Winners see problems and challenges as opportunities to prove what they can do. Winners think positively at all times. That's why problems don't faze them. Winners eat problems and challenges for breakfast. As former NBA coach Pat Riley has said: "If you have a positive attitude and constantly strive to give your best effort, eventually you will overcome your immediate problems and find you are ready for greater challenges."

Corporate speaker Tim Gallwey calls the realm of the mental attitude "the inner game." It's the game you must win, the game that is played between your ears. To win the inner game, you must overcome self-limiting, self-defeating opponents of self-doubt, fear, and laziness. You must prepare yourself mentally by conditioning yourself to think positively. You must continually tell yourself, "I want this! I can do this! Nothing can stop me!" As Kara Leverte Farley and Sheila M. Curry explain in their book *Get Motivated!: Daily Psych-Ups:*

> Something magical happens when we are playing at our optimum ability. Nothing exists except the game. Some people call it playing in "the zone." It doesn't happen all the time, but when it does we feel as if we are in complete control and that we can sense what is going to happen before it does.
>
> Concentration helps us focus and, in effect, turn off our minds. Thinking too much can actually hamper our performance … . Concentrating helps to turn off the mental chatter that can distract us. It can also help to eliminate extra babble—when we are focused we are not thinking about what phone call to return or whether or not we'll have time to pick up our dry cleaning. We are completely involved in our game or our workout. We will discover the time passing without our even noticing.[36]

Australian swimmer Kieren Perkins exemplified this principle by winning Olympic gold in 1992 and 1996, plus the silver in 2000. He achieved his dreams and broke a dozen world records as a distance swimmer. Perkins credits these achievements in large part to his ability to maintain a positive attitude.

"I start months before the event," he says. "I just sit there and visualize the race in my mind. I dive into the pool. I'm swimming strongly. I'm out in front. The crowd [is] roaring, I can hear them. No one can catch me. I even see myself … with the gold medal placed around my neck."[37]

When Perkins competed in the 1996 Summer Olympic Games in Atlanta, he swam a bad qualifying heat in the 1,500-meter freestyle. His disappointing performance shook his confidence. During the 24-hour wait until the final race, he agonized and struggled with self-doubt. He kept picturing himself losing and couldn't focus on a positive attitude.

Kieren Perkins realized that his pessimistic thinking could wreck his Olympic hopes, so he decided to flood his mind with positive thoughts by reading a motivational book. He immersed himself in that book during every waking minute. He didn't set the book down until it was time to suit up for the race. He went into the pool, swam the race— and emerged with a gold medal.

By plunging his mind into a book of positive mental reinforcement, he was able to clear away the pessimism that clouded his thinking. "It's hard to explain," he later told reporters, "but when you are focused you almost have no thought. Sitting behind the blocks I was 100 percent focused and I didn't have a single thing in my mind. I knew what I had to do and it was just a matter of letting my instincts take over."[38]

Call Your Shot

Game 3 of the 1932 World Series was one of the most famous games in baseball history—and it was a powerful demonstration of the power of a positive attitude. The Yankees and Cubs met on October 1, 1932, in Chicago's Wrigley Field. Emotions ran high between the two ball clubs. The Yankees had won the first two games at Yankee Stadium. Now they were on hostile soil, surrounded by 35,000 hate-filled Cubs fans.

Babe Ruth was furious with Chicago because he and his wife had been mobbed, spat upon, and pelted with trash by rioting fans outside his hotel. The morning of the game, Cubs fans had lobbed lemons and other objects at Ruth during batting practice. Cubs trainer Andy Lotshaw had gotten under Ruth's skin by jeering at him and calling him "Potbelly." Babe Ruth was determined to slam the jeers and insults down the throats of the Chicago Cubs and their fans.

In the first inning of the game, Ruth hit a three-run homer. Lou Gehrig hit a homer in the third, bringing the score to 4-0. The Cubs fans responded by throwing more debris at the Yankees. In the fourth inning, the Cubs rebounded, tying the game at 4.

In the fateful fifth inning, Babe Ruth stepped up to the plate. Cubs pitcher Charlie Root wound up and delivered a perfect strike—and Ruth let it go by. He smiled and raised his index finger as if to say, "That's one."

Charlie Root threw two more pitches, ball one and ball two. His next pitch was a fastball down the center of the strike zone. Ruth watched it go by without concern. The crowd roared, knowing that Ruth was one pitch away from a strikeout.

Then Babe Ruth raised his hand and made a gesture that has become enshrined as part of the Babe Ruth legend. He pointed off toward the centerfield fence. He was actually calling his shot, telling Charlie Root, the Chicago Cubs, and all the Cubs fans where he was going to hit the next pitch.

Root went into his windup, then sent the pitch toward the plate, low and away. Ruth swung. Wood and horsehide connected with a sound like a gunshot. The ball soared skyward, over the head of the centerfielder, and deep into the centerfield stands. It landed right where Babe Ruth had predicted it would go—one of the longest homers ever hit at Wrigley Field.

That home run helped send the Yankees to a 7-5 victory over the Cubs. The Yankees ultimately swept the Series. And to this day, sports fans talk about the miracle of Babe Ruth's "called shot," a perfect example of the triumph of a positive attitude over opposition and adversity.

To be the best teammate anybody has ever had, condition yourself to think positively at all times. Have confidence in yourself and your teammates, fire yourself up with enthusiasm, visualize your future success—then call your shot and knock it out of the park.

4

BE A
CHARACTER
PERSON

"Winning takes talent; to repeat takes character."

—Coach John Wooden

John Bryant, one of Jameer Nelson's teammates at St. Joe's, told me that Jameer is:

> the most selfless person I've ever met. He was such a dynamic college basketball player, but not a typical superstar. Jameer was just like the rest of us—a regular guy who happened to be a very good basketball player. He wanted to make all of us look good and make us all successful. He had a major impact on my life through the quality of his character.
>
> Whatever I needed off the court, Jameer would give it to me. My younger brother had the same shoe size as Jameer, so when Jameer stopped wearing a pair of shoes, he'd give them to me to pass along to my brother. After Jameer was drafted by the Magic in 2004, he signed a deal with Converse. For the next few years, Jameer would ship a big box of Converse shoes and gear to me and my family as a gift.

Jameer Nelson is a great teammate because he's a teammate of good character. His character traits include generosity, kindness, compassion, honesty, and integrity. And his character traits also include boldness, mental toughness, self-discipline, hard work, competitive drive, self-reliance, and initiative. A person of good character always demonstrates class, and Jameer is a classy guy. He cares about his teammates and their families, and he represents his team in a professional manner.

People of good character know they are on display 24/7, and they are aware of their influence at all times. You never know who you might run into or who might be watching you, so a person of character never lets down his guard or yields to temptation. That's the kind of character person Jameer Nelson is, and that's another essential ingredient of being the best teammate anybody has ever had.

The Wisdom of Great Coaches

The great coaches will tell you: good character is absolutely essential to the effective functioning of any team.

In July 2009, *The Sporting News* published a list of the 50 greatest coaches of all time, in every sport, at every level, collegiate and professional. The list was compiled by a blue-ribbon committee of sports writers, coaches, and top athletes. The number one coach of all time on that list: John Wooden, who was head basketball coach of the UCLA Bruins from 1948 to 1975. He won 10 NCAA national championships over a 12-year period, including seven championships in a row.

Coach Wooden was famed for being a leader of impeccable character, for recruiting players of good character to his teams, and continually teaching and preaching good character to his teams at every opportunity. In his book *Coach Wooden's Pyramid of Success*, he wrote:

We should be more concerned with our character than with our reputation: Our character is what we truly are, while our reputation is merely what others perceive us to be. As I have often said, having a good reputation doesn't determine success. Neither do awards, accolades, or achievements.

Winning seems so important, but it actually is irrelevant. Having attempted to give it our all is what matters—and we are the only ones who really know the truth about our own capabilities and performance. Did we do our best at this point in our life? Did we leave all we had to give on the field, in the classroom, at the office, or in the trenches? If we did, then we are a success.[39]

In another book, Coach Wooden explained why character is so important in a team setting, and why teammates need to be people of good character:

You might wonder about the connection I see between character and basketball teams or any other kind of team. Character is at the center of what I consider necessary for an individual to be a team player. A person of good character tends to be more considerate of other people—of teammates, for example. A person with character tends to be more giving and sharing with others—with teammates during a game, for example. I believe in passing the ball whenever appropriate and possible. I don't believe a person who is selfish—selfishness is a character issue—would be as willing to pass the ball to a teammate who might then make a basket.[40]

The character of a player has a major impact on team chemistry, coaching strategy, and even winning and losing. A selfish player who hogs the ball and hogs the glory could cost the team a game—and a championship. A teammate with good character, who plays unselfishly for the good of the team instead of for personal glory, could make all the difference between winning and losing. This principle helps to explain why Coach John Wooden, with his focus on character, amassed a winning record that is likely to stand as long as the game of basketball is played.

If Coach Wooden was named the number-one coach of all time by *The Sporting News*, who was number two? It should come as no surprise that the second coach on the list was also intensely committed to recruiting character players and to teaching strong character traits. That coach was Vince Lombardi, the legendary coach of the Green Bay Packers in the 1950s and 1960s. His son, Vince Lombardi, Jr., explained why Coach Lombardi was so focused on the character traits of his players:

Lombardi spoke often of character. His pre-seminary training, his rigorous education at the hands of Fordham's Jesuits, and his sustained immersion in what might be called the "secular religion" of West Point—

where a code of duty and honor prevailed—were immensely influential. This sequence of educational experiences, consistently focused on values, helped him become the man he was. It made him unusually aware of how one goes about building character.

The word "character" is derived from older words that mean "engraved" and "inscribed." These etymological roots imply something important. Character is written, inscribed, and engraved all over you. … Character is founded on unchanging principles. It is your underlying core. It has unspoken power, it is solid and resolute, it doesn't blink. …

Character is not something that is handed to you; it must be forged through years of hard work and discipline. It is the culmination of years of choosing to act one way rather than another, of choosing truth over deception, respect over arrogance, compassion over cruelty. … A favorite theme of Lombardi's was that you cannot simply copy someone else's character. Character must fit our own personality and characteristics if it is to withstand trial by fire.[41]

Vince Lombardi, Jr., has assembled for us some of his father's most profound and practical insights regarding the importance of good character among teammates. Following are a few of those insights in Coach Lombardi's own words:

The most important element in the character makeup is mental toughness.

Mental toughness is humility. Mental toughness is a disciplined will above anything else. What I mean by that is that disciplined will is your own character in action.

Mental toughness is many things and is rather difficult to explain. Its qualities are sacrifice and self-denial. Also, most importantly, it is combined with the perfectly disciplined will, which refuses to give in. It's a state of mind—you could call it "character in action."[42]

Physical toughness will make the opponent weaken, and mental toughness will make him crack.[43]

If Coach Wooden and Coach Lombardi hold the top two spots in *The Sporting News* ranking of all-time greatest coaches, who was third on the list? Answer: Paul "Bear" Bryant, the fabled coach of the Alabama Crimson Tide football program. Like Wooden and Lombardi, Coach Bryant was obsessed with recruiting and teaching good character.

Before coaching at Alabama, Bear Bryant was the head football coach at Texas A&M. One summer day during a preseason practice, he put his 48 players aboard two buses and drove them to a little town called Junction. There, in the middle of nowhere, he put his players through the most punishing training camp in football history. Coach

Bryant's players trained through intense heat, pain, and exhaustion. During that camp, 19 players quit the team and went home. The remaining 29 hung tough and became known as "the Junction boys."

Why did Bear Bryant put his players through such a harsh training camp? Because he wanted to build character. He wanted a team composed entirely of young men who wouldn't quit, who would keep fighting through adversity. His message to his players was a message about character: "Show class, have pride, and display character. If you do, winning takes care of itself."

Bear Bryant also recruited on the basis of character. He once said: "The biggest mistake coaches make is taking borderline cases and trying to save them. I'm not talking about grades now, I'm talking about character."[44]

The great coaches know: great teams are made of great teammates who consistently exemplify good character.

Character Is Influence

Character isn't something you were born with or something that is in your DNA. Character is a *choice*—or perhaps I should say, character is the sum total of *all* the choices you make over your lifetime. Every time you make any moral decision that involves your integrity, honesty, courage, commitment, perseverance, or other character quality, you are either building your character up or tearing it down. Every moral choice either adds to your character or subtracts from it. There are no insignificant decisions.

Character isn't what you say. It's what you do. Many people can say all the right things but their lives betray their words.

Character is crucial to your interaction with your teammates because character produces trust. When your teammates know from their daily interaction with you that you would never lie to them, quit on them, or cheat them, you have built a relationship of trust. Betray that relationship just one time—and you destroy that trust, that relationship. You must have the character to make the right choice 100 percent of the time.

Character is a limiting factor. A person whose character is 100 percent strong 100 percent of the time can achieve almost any height, and can carry his teammates with him. But a person of flawed character is limited in what he can achieve. No one can rise above the limitations of his character.

Good character gives you staying power, because it enables you to endure adversity and persevere through obstacles. Skill and strategy can make you a winner, but only good character can make you a champion over the long haul. When you are facing hardships and trials, when you're exhausted and tempted to quit, only the strength of your character will keep you going and get you across the finish line.

Retired football coach Don Shula led the 1972 Miami Dolphins to the only undefeated season in NFL history. He once said: "Although I realize that I'm not going to win in the NFL without some extraordinary skilled players, character has always been just as important to me—and in some cases, more important."[45]

Tom Coughlin coached the New York Giants to NFL championships in Super Bowl XLII and Super Bowl XLVI. Coughlin agrees that character often outweighs skill as a factor in building a championship team. He writes:

> Character is essential. Essential. Believe me, when you are going to be working closely with someone for a long time, character counts. We have always looked for people who are willing to do whatever is necessary to help the whole organization succeed, rather than being motivated by personal achievement. In our system "we" always supersedes "me." …
>
> There are going to be situations in which character will make a significant difference. When you're dealing with adversity or you have to sacrifice personal achievement for the good of the team or you aren't getting the opportunity you think you've earned, you need to have a personal reservoir of character to draw on. As a coach or a manager, you want to work with dedicated people who have values similar to your own, people you can depend on to be fair when things get tough. The more of those good character people you have in key positions the better chance you have to succeed.[46]

The late Tom Landry coached the Dallas Cowboys to NFL titles in Super Bowl VI and Super Bowl XII. In his autobiography, Landry observed:

> I've seen the difference character makes in individual football players. Give me a choice between an outstanding athlete with poor character and a lesser athlete of good character, and I'll choose the latter every time. The athlete with good character will often perform to his fullest potential and be a successful football player while the outstanding athlete with poor character will usually fail to play up to his potential and often won't even achieve average performance … . In my opinion, character is the most important determinant of a person's success, achievement, and ability to handle adversity.[47]

Tom Landry learned the importance of character in his players through the hard knocks of experience. He recalled:

> When I first started coaching I thought mostly of physical ability; quickness, agility, control, strength, and explosiveness. Then, as we developed into a stronger team, character became more important. The character and competitiveness of a player become the more controlling

factors. When you reach a championship level, what separates you is basically the character on your team. If you have enough character, it'll usually pull you out of tough situations.[48]

Because character is an increasingly rare quality in this world, your example of good character sets you apart from the crowd. Good character makes you a role model and a leader to be followed and emulated. Your teammates will look up to you if you demonstrate good character all the time.

Character is influence. And influence makes you a leader.

Wear Your Character Like a Medal

Coach Vince Lombardi said: "Character, rather than education, is man's greatest need and man's greatest safeguard, because character is higher than intellect."[49]

Dayton Moore, general manager of the Kansas City Royals, said:

> Character is the most important thing when putting together a baseball team. The players are together for 162 games throughout the course of the year. And for nine months out of a year, they have to like being around each other. Every successful team, every successful organization, every successful situation I have been in, we've had a group of people who have had the ability to put others first, and … put their own needs and wants and desires second.[50]

Where does the motivation come from to make good character choices? For most people of good character, that motivation must be instilled early in life. Good character can be learned later in life, but it's rare that a person of poor character becomes a person of good character overnight. When a person of poor character suddenly embraces the traits of good character, it is usually because of a spiritual conversion or a "moment of clarity," such as when an alcoholic "hits bottom" and goes into Alcoholics Anonymous to get "clean and sober." The development of good character is usually a long—in fact, a lifelong—process of growth and gradual change.

The story of George Herman "Babe" Ruth is the story of a young man who started out without any training or role models for good character. He told his own story in an article that appeared in the October 1948 issue of *Guideposts* magazine. The article he wrote is so important and fascinating that I've decided to include a lengthy excerpt of it. He wrote as follows:

> Don't get the idea that I'm proud of my harum-scarum youth. I'm not. I simply had a rotten start in life, and it took me a long time to get my bearings. Looking back to my youth, I honestly don't think I knew the difference between right and wrong. I spent much of my early boyhood

living over my father's saloon in Baltimore—and when I wasn't living over it, I was in it, soaking up the atmosphere. I hardly knew my parents.

St. Mary's Industrial School in Baltimore, where I was finally taken, has been called an orphanage and a reform school. It was, in fact, a training school for orphans, incorrigibles, delinquents and runaways picked up on the streets of the city. I was listed as an incorrigible. I guess I was. Perhaps I would always have been but for Brother Matthias, the greatest man I have ever known … .

I doubt if any appeal could have straightened me out except a Power over and above man—the appeal of God. Iron-rod discipline couldn't have done it. Nor all the punishment and reward systems that could have been devised. God had an eye out for me, just as He has for you, and He was pulling for me to make the grade … .

I got one thing straight (and I wish all kids did)—that God was Boss. He was not only my Boss but Boss of all my bosses. Up till then, like all bad kids, I hated most of the people who had control over me and could punish me. I began to see that I had a higher Person to reckon with who never changed, whereas my earthly authorities changed from year to year. Those who bossed me had the same self-battles—they, like me, had to account to God. I also realized that God was not only just, but merciful. He knew we were weak and that we all found it easier to be stinkers than good sons of God, not only as kids but all through our lives. …

I've seen a great number of "he-men" in my baseball career, but never one equal to Brother Matthias. He stood six feet six and weighed 250 pounds. It was all muscle. He could have been successful at anything—and he chose the church.

It was he who introduced me to baseball. Very early he noticed that I had some natural talent for throwing and catching. He used to back me in a corner of the big yard at St. Mary's and bunt a ball to me by the hour, correcting the mistakes I made. … Thanks to Brother Matthias I was able to leave St. Mary's in 1914 and begin my professional career with the famous Baltimore Orioles. …

I strayed from the Church, but I don't think I forgot my religious training. I just overlooked it. I prayed often and hard, but like many irrepressible young fellows, the swift tempo of living shoved religion into the background. …

As far as I'm concerned, and I think as far as most kids go, once religion sinks in, it stays there—deep down. The lads who get religious training, get it where it counts—in the roots. They may fail it, but it never fails them. When the score is against them, or they get a bum pitch, that unfailing Something inside will be there to draw on. I've seen it with kids. I know from the letters they write me. The more I think of it, the more important I feel it is to give kids "the works" as far as religion is concerned. They'll never want to be holy—they'll act like tough monkeys in contrast, but somewhere inside will be a solid little chapel. It may get dusty from neglect, but the time will come when the door will be opened with much relief. But the kids can't take it, if we don't give it to them. ... All through the years, even when the big money was rolling in, I'd never forget St. Mary's, Brother Matthias and the boys I left behind. I kept going back.

As I look back at those moments when I let the kids down—they were my worst. I guess I was so anxious to enjoy life to the fullest that I forgot the rules or ignored them. Once in a while you can get away with it, but not for long. When I broke training, the effects were felt by myself and by the ball team—and even by the fans.

While I drifted away from the Church, I did have my own "altar," a big window of my New York apartment overlooking the city lights. Often I would kneel before that window and say my prayers. I would feel quite humble then. I'd ask God to help me not make such a big fool of myself and pray that I'd live up to what He expected of me.

In December, 1946, I was in French Hospital, New York, facing a serious operation. Paul Carey, one of my oldest and closest friends, was by my bed one night. "They're going to operate in the morning, Babe," Paul said. "Don't you think you ought to put your house in order?"

I didn't dodge the long, challenging look in his eyes. I knew what he meant. For the first time I realized that death might strike me out. I nodded, and Paul got up, called in a Chaplain, and I made a full confession. ...

As I lay in bed that evening I thought to myself what a comforting feeling to be free from fear and worries. I now could simply turn them over to God. Later on, my wife brought in a letter from a little kid in Jersey City. "Dear Babe," he wrote, "Everybody in the seventh grade class is pulling and praying for you. I am enclosing a medal, which if you wear it will make you better. Your pal—Mike Quinlan. P.S. I know this will be your 61st homer. You'll hit it."

I asked them to pin the Miraculous Medal to my pajama coat. I've worn the medal constantly ever since. I'll wear it to my grave.[51]

Babe Ruth was battling brain cancer at Memorial Sloan-Kettering Cancer Center in Manhattan when he wrote those words with the help of some friends. The manuscript arrived at the *Guideposts* editorial office on August 16, 1948—the same day Babe Ruth died in his sleep at age 53.

As Babe Ruth alluded to in the article, he had not always led an exemplary life. Throughout his baseball career, he drank too much and he was something of a womanizer—but it was also said that he never took advantage of an innocent young girl and he never coaxed a teammate into corrupt behavior. He was a human being with feet of clay, but he left this world as a man of faith—and yes, I believe he left as a man of character, taking one last opportunity to use his influence for the good of others.

How are you influencing your teammates through the impact of your character? To be the best teammate anybody has ever had, demonstrate good character consistently. Exemplify good character when you are with your teammates and when you are all alone. Be a teammate of consistent good character, and wear your character like a medal throughout your life.

5 RESPONSIBLE
BE

"Your responsibility to your teammates is to play the best that you can play as an individual, yet not take anything away from being part of a team."

—Retired Hockey Player Wayne Gretzky

nickp37/iStock/Thinkstock

Phil Martelli, Jameer Nelson's coach at St. Joseph's, told me about the way Jameer took personal responsibility for his teammates. "If I got on a kid during practice," Phil said, "Jameer would often step in and say, 'Coach, I've got it.' Then he'd start to work with this player to help him. As great a basketball player as Jameer was, he was an even greater teammate—the best teammate ever. Jameer took responsibility to coach and motivate his teammates at St. Joe's, and they all took their lead from him."

A great teammate takes personal responsibility. He never engages in blaming others, making excuses, or avoiding the work that needs to be done. A great teammate steps up and says, "This is my responsibility. I've got it. Trust me to get it done."

A few years ago, the great Boston Celtics center Bill Russell wrote a book called *Russell Rules: 11 Lessons on Leadership from the Twentieth Century's Greatest Winner*. What was the very first of Bill Russell's 11 rules?

> *Rule One:* Take responsibility for everything you do. One great quality that leaders have is the ability to take responsibility—we all know that responsibility ultimately gravitates to the person who can shoulder it. We must all be strong enough. The more you stand behind what you do or what you decide, the more you will be able to feel that is a reflection of yourself. It is your integrity that is at stake when you genuinely take responsibility for what you do.[52]

And Pat Summitt, the great former basketball coach of the University of Tennessee Lady Volunteers, agrees:

> If you don't want responsibility, don't sit in the big chair. That's the deal. To be successful, you must accept full responsibility. For everything. Headaches, problems, crises. Even when it doesn't seem fair. And here's part two: The more successful you are, the more responsibility you must assume. Responsibility never ends. It's not a step. Or just a chapter. You don't finish it and then move on to something more fun or interesting. Responsibility is a constant state of being.[53]

You cannot evade or avoid your own responsibility without shifting that responsibility to someone else, usually your teammate. To be the best teammate anybody has ever had, shoulder your own responsibility and demonstrate a responsible attitude at all times. Be more concerned with accepting responsibility than with assigning blame. People of weak character dread accepting responsibility, but a willingness to be responsible and accountable truly makes us mature men and women—and great teammates.

Where Does a Sense of Responsibility Come From?

In the early years of the Michael Jordan era of the Chicago Bulls, the sports world was abuzz over this dominant NBA star. Many sportswriters suggested that Jordan wasn't being paid enough, and he needed to hold out and force the Bulls to renegotiate his contract and raise his salary. But Michael Jordan's mother disagreed.

I remember seeing a TV interview with Deloris Jordan. She told the interviewer: "I've talked to Michael, and I told him not to listen to all that talk. I said, 'Michael, you signed a contract. You gave your word and your word is your bond. When you signed that contract, you didn't know if your team would be great or terrible. It's turned out well, and if the owners decide to rewrite your contract and give you a bonus, that's fine. But in the meantime, you need to honor your word and live up to your responsibility.'"

The great college football coach Lou Holtz learned about responsibility when he was in junior high. I once saw him tell this story to a TV interviewer:

> I had an English teacher named Miss Dunlop. She was a little five-foot one-inch hundred-pound woman, and pound for pound, the meanest person I've ever met. She was hard on us, and she made sure we knew the rules of English. My friends and I would make fun of her outside of class, but as I got older and wiser, I realized what a great teacher she was. The best teachers aren't the ones who coddle you but the ones who challenge you. Miss Dunlop challenged us to take personal responsibility. She taught us that it was our responsibility to be prepared, and we couldn't shift the blame to anyone else. Down through the years, wherever I have coached, the spirit of Miss Dunlop has been right there beside me, reminding me to teach my players to do what is right and shoulder their own responsibility.

Cal Ripken, Jr., the Iron Man of baseball, played in the Major League for 21 years, all of them for the Baltimore Orioles (1981–2001). As a shortstop and third baseman, he racked up many notable accomplishments, but he is best known for breaking Lou Gehrig's record for consecutive games played—a 17-year streak of 2,632 games that ended in 1998. Ripken's streak is evidence of a deeply rooted sense of responsibility to the game and to his teammates. Where did that character trait of responsibility come from? Ripken explained:

> I was shaped and molded by my dad, that it's a sense of responsibility to be a player and come to the ballpark and play every day. ... There were stories that my dad as a catcher would have, where he'd get a foul ball hit off his finger and his finger would split open, you know? And even Earl Weaver, who managed my dad in the minor leagues, would come out and say, come on, Rip, we've got to take you out of here.
>
> He'd say ... Put a little tape on this and I'll keep playing. That was the sort of stories I grew up with. ...
>
> [The streak] didn't happen because I wanted it to happen and it was not my life goal to do that. It was a by-product of doing what I thought

was the right thing. And what I thought was the right thing came from my dad, who said, you as a baseball player have a responsibility, you know, to the team. ...

Sure, there were days I didn't feel like playing. ... But I thought there was an honor to being part of the team and a sense of obligation and responsibility.[54]

In short, Ripken's goal was not the streak. His goal was to live out his sense of responsibility. The streak was just a natural consequence of a life responsibly lived.

John Mitchell is a defensive line coach and assistant head coach for the Pittsburgh Steelers. In his college days, he was the first African-American to play football for Coach Bear Bryant at Alabama. He later became the first black assistant coach at Alabama.

"When I went to Alabama," Mitchell recalls, "I was a little nineteen-year-old kid that didn't know anything. Coach Bryant made me grow up to accept responsibility. He told me once when I was struggling and thinking about quitting, 'If you quit this time, you won't even think about it the second time.' That has stayed with me to this day, and I never think about quitting anything. I'd rather die than quit, and I tell the players I coach the same thing."[55]

J.C. Watts was born and raised in Eufaula, Oklahoma, and played quarterback for the Sooners of the University of Oklahoma. He was later elected to the House of Representatives, where he served from 1995 to 2003 as the congressman from Oklahoma's 4th Congressional District. He recalls learning responsibility growing up in Eufaula. In his 2002 book, he wrote:

Outside Washington, people are a whole lot more concerned about a late Social Security check than the latest political scandal. They want to know what you're going to do to help their kids learn to read and write, not whether you lean to the right or the left. ...

The value system in Eufaula was much the same. Your word mattered a lot more than how much money you had in your pocket. Your honesty was more important than the house you lived in or the car you drove. ... In my family, we learned early on that personal responsibility was the only direct route to the "promised land," and you didn't get respect unless you earned it. ... I understood at a very young age that each of us is responsible for our actions and ourselves. ...

I believe in these values—not just for any one ethnic group, but for our nation as a whole. They guide us to a better place for ourselves and our families.[56]

The sense of responsibility described by Deloris Jordan, Lou Holtz, Cal Ripken, John Mitchell, and J.C. Watts is all too rare in today's world. Most people, it seems, only want to take credit when decisions turn out well. When a plan or decision fails, it's hard to find anyone to accept responsibility.

I don't know about you, but I would hate to be on a team filled with finger-pointers and blame-shifters. I want to be on a team where my teammates all take personal responsibility for their actions, their decisions, and their mistakes. I want to be on a team where no one makes excuses, where all of my teammates possess the character trait of responsibility. And most of all, I want to be that kind of responsible leader and friend to all of my teammates.

The Rule of the River

In 1965, when Duke University basketball coach Mike Krzyzewski was a lowly plebe at West Point, he was introduced to an academy tradition the cadets called "Beast Barracks." For two months, the upperclassmen would haze the plebes and strip them of their individual identity. Young Mike Krzyzewski learned quickly that there were only three possible answers when an upperclassman asked him a question: "Yes, sir," "No, sir," or "No excuse, sir."

One day, Krzyzewski was walking on campus in full uniform, accompanied by his roommate. The roommate stepped in a puddle and some of the mud spattered Krzyzewski's freshly-shined shoes. Moments later, Krzyzewski heard an upperclassman shout, "Halt!"

Krzyzewski stopped in his tracks. Two upperclassmen approached, looking Mike and his roommate up and down. One pointed to the roommate and said, "You're okay." The other squinted at Mike's name tag, trying to decipher the word KRZYZEWSKI. "What kind of name is that?" the upperclassman asked.

It was a question that could not be answered "Yes, sir," "No, sir," or "No excuse, sir," so Krzyzewski remained silent.

"Your shoes are a mess," one upperclassman said.

Krzyzewski wished he could blame his roommate for splashing mud on his shoes, but that would be ducking personal responsibility. So, still standing at attention, Krzyzewski said, "No excuse, sir."

The upperclassman barked insults at him, then wrote him up, giving him demerits for his mud-splashed shoes. Initially, Krzyzewski was furious with his roommate for the trouble he was in—but after a few minutes, his attitude changed. Krzyzewski recalled:

> When my roommate stepped in that puddle and splashed mud on my shoes, I had a choice to make. Do I continue or do I go back and change my shoes? What my roommate did was something I had no control over. But the next event was my decision to make. They were

my shoes and I was responsible for them. I kept walking and took the chance that I wouldn't be caught. I could have gone back but I didn't. That was my choice. The truth is that I had no right to be mad at my roommate. I should have been mad at myself. And later, when I understood the reality of the situation, I *was* angry with myself. That was a huge lesson for me.

So how does that lesson translate to what I do now is a coach, as a leader?

Well, no matter what happens, it's my team. I'm responsible. There's no excuse.[57]

The muddy shoes incident was a turning point in Mike Krzyzewski's character growth and leadership development. He learned a valuable lesson in taking responsibility for his own actions. He has carried that lesson throughout his coaching career.

Mike Westhoff retired in 2012 as special teams coach for the New York Jets. In 1989, when he was 40 years old and working as special teams coach of Don Shula's Miami Dolphins, Westhoff was diagnosed with cancer. His surgeons removed an egg-sized tumor from his left femur (thigh bone).

A few years ago, I interviewed Mike Westhoff, and he told me: "You really find out what you're made of when you're diagnosed with a life-threatening disease. Fighting bone cancer changed my life. It took eight major surgeries to help me beat the cancer. One of those surgeries saved my leg from being amputated." The surgeons used two metal plates, 25 screws, and a seven-inch piece of bone from a deceased donor to repair his femur.

"I didn't want to sit around and think about how sick I was," Mike said. "Everything is still there—your job, family and friends, stress and bills. How do you handle all of these issues as well as the cancer? I had to dig deep and find new strengths within myself in order to beat the cancer."

Mike told Coach Shula he wanted to stay on the job right through his regimen of chemotherapy. Shula said, "Fine, let's get back to work." Westhoff continued:

Coach Shula wasn't going to go easy on me just because I was sick. He's an intense coach, and he has high demands for his staff and players. While I was battling cancer, Coach was supportive, but he didn't treat me any differently than he had before. He treated me the way I *could* be, not the way I was. He never looked at me as if I was handicapped. That helped me to see myself as Coach Shula saw me—not a guy on his back in a hospital bed, but as a coach who was going to get the job done. That, as much as anything, helped me get past the cancer.

When Mike Westhoff came to the Dolphin's pre-season training camp, he was pale, thin, bald from the chemo, and walking on crutches. Nevertheless, he went straight to work as if he was as healthy as ever.

"It's all about responsibility," he told me. "I'm responsible to do my job, and I'm responsible for my own recovery. Going through that experience has made me a better coach. I preach and teach personal responsibility to my players. They're accountable to learn the system and to execute it correctly. As a result, my teams have traditionally been among the least penalized teams in the NFL."

As part of his recovery, Mike took on new physical challenges. He said:

> I went white water rafting on the Snake River in Wyoming. Each raft holds six or eight people. The guide explained that if someone got thrown from the raft, all attention must be directed toward rescuing that person.
>
> But the guide also explained something called "the rule of the river," which states that if you fall into the water, you must be active in your own rescue. You can't just sit there in the water waiting for someone to pull you out. Do that and you may end up floating all the way to Mexico. You must take personal responsibility and work with your fellow rafters to get back to safety.
>
> Responsibility in the NFL operates like the rule of the river. Every player must know and execute his assignment. If one teammate fails to shoulder his share of the load, even for one down, the whole team effort collapses.

The rule of the river is also the rule of the football field, the rule of the cancer ward, and the rule of whatever arena you play in. Your teammates are there to help you, and you're there to help your teammates. They are counting on you to be responsible and to shoulder your share of the load.

You can't run away from your problems, and you can't run away from yourself. The wise thing to do is to accept personal responsibility for solving your problems and, yes, the problems of the team. Great teammates say, "I am responsible for my attitude, my decisions, my actions, and my mistakes. You can depend on me, because I will never shift the blame to anyone else."

To be the best teammate anybody has ever had, be a teammate who accepts personal responsibility.

6

BE A
LEADER

"Leadership is unlocking people's potential to become better."

—Former NBA Star Bill Bradley

Fuse/Thinkstock

Rodney Powell, longtime equipment manager and traveling secretary for the Orlando Magic, told me a story about the leadership ability of Jameer Nelson:

> Jameer arrived here in 2004 and as a rookie he had the instinct not to be a follower, but a leader. He observed some of our veteran players who led the wrong way and he wanted to move the team in the right direction. He had a different mindset.
>
> Here of late, we have a very young team and Jameer is the ultimate team leader for those younger teammates. He has set out to be a good influence on the young guys. He wants to be a good teacher and mentor for them—a role model who leads by example. Jameer has always been the leader of our team and he's setting just the right tone.

To be the best teammate anybody has ever had, you've got to be a good leader on the field, in the locker room, and in your personal life. A great teammate is a good leader.

Back in my days as a baseball catcher in college and in the minor leagues, there were very few books written about leadership. There was no leadership training in the corporate or academic world as there is today. In fact, the word "leadership" was seldom studied or discussed back in my younger days. So I never studied leadership in school and never received any formal leadership training.

Yet, as a young athlete at Tower Hill School in Wilmington, Delaware, I naturally gravitated toward leadership roles. I was the quarterback on the football team, the catcher on the baseball team, the point guard on the basketball team. I accepted leadership roles almost as if leadership was expected of me. No one tapped me on the shoulder and said, "Okay, you're the leader." It just seemed to be a natural fit for me.

When I attended Wake Forest University in North Carolina, I was the catcher on the baseball team and active in the letterman's association. Every year, the letterman's group, called the Monogram Club, staged a freshman-varsity basketball game. Less than a week before the game was to be held, Jerry Steele, president of the club, poked his forefinger at my solar plexus and said, "Williams, you're in charge of the freshman-varsity game."

I had less than a week to print up the tickets, arrange for a halftime show, and launch a promotional blitz. I went around to my teammates, my fellow Monogram Clubbers, and I delegated tasks: "You're in charge of this! You take care of that! Move it!" I assembled my team, put them in motion, and the entire event came off perfectly. It was an evening of crowd-pleasing entertainment that garnered rave reviews.

The next morning, I woke up and my first thought was, *Hey, I could do this as a career!* As it turned out, I've spent the past 50 years in professional sports doing pretty much the same thing I did when I assembled that Monogram Club basketball game. For more than five decades, I've been putting teams together, putting on shows, drawing crowds to games, and promoting like crazy. In short, I've been a leader.

When Jerry Steele poked his finger into my chest and put me in charge, he launched me on a career path I had never even thought of before. I had always wanted a career in sports, but I had seen myself as a baseball player in the major leagues. That experience helped prepare me for a different kind of career in sports—a leadership role, first in minor league baseball, and later in the National Basketball Association.

The Seven Sides of Leadership

Over the years, I've made an intensive study of leadership, and I have become convinced that the essential principles of leadership can be distilled to seven fundamental ingredients. All of us are born with at least one or two of these ingredients, and the rest can be studied, practiced, and learned. If you have all seven of these ingredients—what I call The Seven Sides of Leadership—then you have what it takes to be a leader among your teammates. Those seven ingredients are as follows:

1. Vision
2. Communication
3. People Skills
4. Character
5. Competence
6. Boldness
7. A Serving Heart

These seven ingredients produce magical results every time they are applied. Jameer Nelson has all seven of these ingredients—and that's a key reason why he is such a great teammate. You can have all seven as well. Let's take a closer look at look at The Seven Sides of Leadership.

The First Side of Leadership: Vision

"You'd better have a vision," said Coach Lou Holtz. "You'd better have a plan, and you'd better have the passion for getting things done." This is great advice for anyone who seeks to be a leader at any level in a team environment. The purpose of leadership is to organize and motivate people to work together to achieve important goals. Vision is the ability to look into the future and imagine those goals.

I discovered the concept of vision when I was a 24-year-old general manager of a Minor League baseball team in Spartanburg, South Carolina. I had never taken on such a big challenge before, and I wasn't sure I was up to the task. When I got my first eye-full of our ballpark, my heart sank. The place was a decaying eyesore. It almost seemed that the paint was peeling and the weeds were growing right before my eyes. I wondered, "What have I gotten myself into?"

Then I let my imagination run wild. I pictured that ballpark in the summertime, with the playing field freshly manicured, the walls and stands neatly painted, and the bleachers packed with cheering fans. That mental image became my vision. For weeks, as I worked 16-hour days, that vision sustained and motivated me.

On opening day, 5,000 people passed through the gates at our little field of dreams. We drew record crowds that summer. And as I looked around at that ballpark, which I had painted, repaired, mowed, and manicured with my own hands, I knew that the reality matched my vision in every detail.

Years later, I went on to bigger visions, such as my dream of assembling an NBA championship team in Philadelphia. In 1983, that vision became a reality as the Philadelphia 76ers won the NBA Finals.

Then, in 1986, I moved my family from Philadelphia to Orlando to chase an even bigger vision—the dream of founding an NBA expansion franchise in the center of Florida, the Orlando Magic. We started without a lot of money, without a fan base, without an arena, without a pro sports tradition in that city, and without any commitment from the NBA. But working closely with local business leaders, I fought hard for that vision, and today that vision is a reality.

Vision is the fountainhead of leadership. Everything else you accomplish as a leader flows from your vision of the future.

The Second Side of Leadership: Communication

What good is a vision if you can't *communicate* your vision to your teammates? Vision alone is not enough to get the job done. Through your communication skills, you are able to share your vision with your teammates, so that they will become as excited and motivated as you are.

Jon Gruden, former head coach of the Oakland Raiders and the Tampa Bay Buccaneers, learned the importance of clear communication from his coaching mentor, Mike Holmgren. He observes that Holmgren's background as a high school teacher prepared him to be a great communicator to his players. Holmgren would turn complex plays into a series of step-by-step instructions that his players could easily follow and execute. Gruden said that Coach Holmgren "had a knack for conveying his thoughts in twenty-five words or less. He didn't start rambling and talking about things that were irrelevant to the question that you had just asked. He was always to the point."

As a result, Holmgren's players knew their assignments and carried them out according to the game plan. Most important of all, Holmgren communicated confidence to his players. Gruden concluded:

> When [Coach Holmgren] installs a game plan, showing each play and its corresponding number on the overhead projector, he always exudes confidence.

"Picture Number 73 is going to be a touchdown Sunday," he'd say matter-of-factly, about a pass play designed to have Joe [Montana] throw to Jerry Rice, who would just blow past some poor DB trying to cover him one-on-one over the middle. "Pay attention, men. It's 76 X Shallow Cross. Roger's going in motion to the weak side. The free safety is going to jump the tight end on the hook route, and Jerry Rice is going to be there for a touchdown. It's going to happen, man. Circle it now. Star it. It's a touchdown."

I would sit there and go, "Man, it's seven to nothing already. What's the next picture?"

But that's how you install plays. Confident. Concise. Crystal-clear. No one does it better than Mike Holmgren.[58]

To be an effective leader on your team, focus on communicating clearly, confidently, and concisely so that your teammates understand. Avoid jargon or big words meant to impress. Just say what you mean, and mean what you say.

Communicate to spread optimism and enthusiasm among your teammates. Your confidence will fire up your teammates to overcome obstacles and achieve big goals. As General Colin Powell once said, "Perpetual optimism is a force multiplier."[59] When you communicate optimism to your teammates, you multiply their mental, emotional, and physical energy—and that increases your team's advantage over the opponent.

Celtics legend Bill Russell recalls a 1968 playoff game against the Celts' most bitter rivals, the 76ers. Facing elimination, Russell and the Celtics clung to a scant two-point lead as the game wound down. With 12 seconds remaining, the 76ers fouled Russell. If he simply made his two free-throws, the Celtics were nearly certain to put the game away (in those days, there was no three-point shot). If Russell missed both shots, however, the 76ers had a chance to tie it up and take the game into overtime.

Russell went to the line and launched his first shot. He missed.

One of Bill Russell's teammates, guard Sam Jones, went to Russell's side, leaned close to his ear, and said a few words.

Moments later, Russell launched his second shot—and drained it. When time expired, the Celtics were victorious—and they had escaped elimination. Bill Russell and the Celtics went on to beat the 76ers in the division finals, then beat the Lakers in the finals for the NBA championship.

What were the inspiring words Sam Jones said before Bill Russell made that all-important free-throw? He said, "Flex your knees, Bill." In *Russell Rules*, Bill Russell explained:

When I shot fouls successfully, I always flexed my knees. When I missed, I was most often stiff-legged. "Flex your knees, Bill," was the inspirational word I got from him at that last, crucial moment. It was about as inspiring as a car manual, but it was the only thing I needed to hear at that moment for us to win.[60]

Sam Jones was an Ultimate Teammate, who communicated exactly what Bill Russell needed to hear at just the right time. Great teammates communicate to motivate and inspire, and they enable their teammates to achieve their goals.

The Third Side of Leadership: People Skills

Theodore Roosevelt once said, "The most important single ingredient in the formula of success is knowing how to get along with people." Great teammates have big hearts for other people. They have empathy and compassion for their fellow players. To be the Ultimate Teammate, you've got to love the people on your team.

The great coaches know how important it is to love their players and care about their needs. Eddie Robinson, the longtime football coach at Grambling State University, said in his autobiography, "You can't coach a person unless you love him. I loved these guys and looked at them as though they were the ones I wanted to marry my daughter."[61]

I once spoke at an event in Charlotte, North Carolina, and in the course of my talk, I quoted those words by Coach Eddie Robinson. After my talk, a woman came up to me and said, "In the late 1990s, I was sitting in a waiting room at the Green Clinic in Ruston, Louisiana, not far from the Grambling campus. I noticed that Coach Eddie Robinson was also in the waiting room. So I spoke to him and said, 'Coach, what advice would you have for someone like me?' He said, 'Love everybody—and do it out loud.' I thought that was the best advice I'd ever heard. Now, I'm not a tattoo gal, but I do carry this reminder of what Coach Robinson said to me that day."

She pulled up her sleeve and showed me a tattoo on her right wrist. It was such a tiny tattoo that I had to put on my reading glasses to see it. There were no words, just a tiny little heart. She said, "It's just a reminder of Coach Robinson's words to me, 'Love everybody—and do it out loud.' I've been trying to follow his advice ever since."

You can't be a great teammate unless you love all your teammates and love them out loud. You don't have to *like* your teammate, but you do have to *love* your teammate. You may wonder: "How can I love people without liking them?" Let's be clear about the meaning of the word *love*.

The ancient Greeks used four different words to express four different kinds of love. The particular form of love I'm talking about here—love that is a deliberate decision of the will—is a love the ancient Greeks called *agape* (pronounced "uh-GAW-pay"). *Agape*-love is a deliberate commitment to show love to someone who is not particularly lovable. It's sometimes called "unconditional love." This kind of love means you've got to seek the best for your teammates even when they mess up and disappoint you. It means you have to forgive the unforgivable. It means you love them in spite of racial differences, cultural differences, political differences, religious differences, and different sexual orientation.

This doesn't mean you have to act touchy-feely around them or indulge and tolerate their weaknesses. Sometimes, the most loving thing you can do for others is to be firm and tough with them, to confront them when they mess up or slack off. But no matter what that person does, you always seek what's best for that person, even if it means you must sacrifice your own wants, wishes, and needs.

Coach John Wooden of UCLA was a man with great people skills and a great love for his players. Swen Nater, who played for Coach John Wooden in the early 1970s, told me that Coach Wooden once told his former players, "I didn't *like* you all the same, but I tried to *love* you all the same." The love Coach Wooden spoke of was *agape*-love, rooted in a decision, not in the emotions.

Vince Lombardi understood the power of love among teammates. He said, "When those tough sportswriters asked me what made the Packers click, I said, 'Love.' It was the kind [of love] that means loyalty, teamwork, respecting the dignity of another—heart power, not hate power."[62] Love is a people skill—one of the most vital skills any teammate can have.

The other important people skills, of course, that can help make you the best teammate anybody has ever had include the following abilities:
- To listen to teammates and really hear what they mean
- To empathize with teammates and their struggles
- To tolerate different opinions, personalities, and ways of doing things
- To be patient with teammates who lag behind
- To negotiate with others and resolve conflict
- To be courteous and kind to everyone without prejudice
- To level with your teammates and always tell the truth

The people skill of honesty is especially important for building trust on your team. Hall of Fame baseball manager George "Sparky" Anderson once said, "The most important thing is to be honest with [teammates]. If you do that, they'll be yours. But if a player finds you've lied to him, you'll not only lose him but ten others in the clubhouse."[63]

An Ultimate Teammate is a leader with excellent people skills, including the skills of unconditional love and unconditional honesty.

The Fourth Side of Leadership: Character

We already looked at character in Chapter 4, so I'll be brief and start with a personal story. I was 13 when I learned an important lesson about character. I tried out for a summer sandlot baseball team, and was chosen as the youngest player on the team. Because all the other players were older than I was, I wondered if I could compete at their level.

My mother and grandmother drove me to my first game. They sat in the front seat; I sat in the back seat. During the drive, we talked about some of the challenges I would likely face as the youngest player on the team. At one point, I said, "Well, if it doesn't work out, I can always quit."

Instantly, my grandmother turned and glared at me. "You! Don't! Quit!" she said. "Nobody in this family quits!"

That shocked me, but I got the message. After all, what kind of teammate would I be if I simply quit when the going got rough?

It was a summer of adversity, and I had to work hard to keep up with the older players—but I *didn't quit*. After that message from my grandmother, I didn't dare quit—and I'm grateful to this day for her stern and unyielding message. That early lesson in the character trait of perseverance has been the foundation for everything I have accomplished in my life, from youth sports to being a Minor League Baseball executive to being a general manager in the NBA to cofounding the Orlando Magic.

Anytime the going got rough in my career and I felt like giving up, I could hear my grandmother say, "You! Don't! Quit!" And I never have. Character—especially the character quality of perseverance—is essential to being a great teammate.

The Fifth Side of Leadership: Competence

Larry Bird once said, "Leadership is diving for a loose ball, getting the crowd involved, getting other players involved. It's being able to take it as well as dish it out. That's the only way you're going to get respect from the players." He is talking about the character quality of competence, the ability to compete at the highest possible level, physically, mentally, and emotionally.

Competence can also be defined as the ability to solve problems. I learned this lesson in my early career as a general manager of a Minor League Baseball team in Spartanburg, South Carolina. Minor League Baseball is all about problems and problem-solving. The entire season was one crisis after another. Unexpected weather would rain out my big promotional efforts, or the Phillies front office would snatch up our best player and move him to a higher level. Sometimes, my problems with the team seemed insoluble, so I would take them to the team's co-owner, Mr. R.E. Littlejohn, spread them out on his desk, and ask for help.

I can still hear his gentle South Carolina drawl as he said, "It'll be good for you to solve this problem on your own, Pat. Don't run from your problems. When you solve them yourself, you have a wonderful opportunity to sell yourself to others by proving that you are a problem-solver."

Another crucial competency is team-building. People are social beings. We are designed to meet challenges and achieve goals through teamwork. Mike Krzyzewski once said: "People want to be on a team. They want to be part of something bigger than themselves. They want to be in a situation where they feel that they are doing something for the greater good."[64]

Coach Bill Curry was the architect of the Georgia State University football program from 2008 to 2012, and has also coached at Georgia Tech, Alabama, and Kentucky. He calls teamwork "the miracle of the huddle" because when a group of diverse people come together and fuse themselves into a team, their individual differences are miraculously transcended. Curry explains: "In that huddle is Black America and White America, liberal and conservative, Jew and Gentile, Muslim and atheist, West Coast and East Coast, North and South. ... We put 'em in the same color shirt, and we make 'em run and sweat and bleed. ... And it begins to occur to everyone the sweat smells about the same on everybody. When I get busted in the mouth, my blood is about the same color as my brother's here. So the privilege of stepping into that huddle becomes transforming."[65]

Teamwork is the power to leverage individual competencies and combine them into a force that far exceeds the sum of their parts. To be a great teammate, develop the competency of team-building.

Another key competency is the ability to maintain your poise under pressure and in times of unfair treatment. Walt Frazier had a 13-year career in the NBA—10 years with the Knicks, and three with the Cavaliers—before retiring in 1980. He was never charged with a technical foul in his long and remarkable career. In his book *The Game Within the Game*, Frazier explains why:

> When a ref made a poor call on me, I never talked back. ... To me, a look is worth a thousand words. I'd just put my hands on my hips and fix the ref with a look that said, "You stupid guy. What are you doing?" but I'd never say a word. I kept my emotions within. I kept my cool because I knew that I couldn't look like I was losing it. I was the leader on the floor and the other players on the Knicks—as well as Red Holzman, our coach—looked to me to keep my cool. ...
>
> When I was in the eighth grade—when everything would be in disarray on the court and my team started to discombobulate—my coach would pull me over and say, "Frazier, don't lose your head, son. Your brains are in it." It was funny, but I never forgot those words of wisdom.[66]

A competent player can maintain poise in adversity, even the adversity of an obviously bad call. Competence is a crucial leadership trait and a quality that every great teammate must have. Your competence qualifies you to lead in any situation.

The Sixth Side of Leadership: Boldness

"The topic of leadership is a touchy one," Kobe Bryant once said. "A lot of leaders fail because they don't have the bravery to touch that nerve or strike that chord. Throughout my years, I haven't had that fear." Every great teammate must be a leader, and every great leader must be bold.

When legendary Packers quarterback Bart Starr entered his senior year in high school, his coach, Bill Moseley, arranged for him to be personally tutored by Kentucky quarterback Vito "Babe" Parilli. For two weeks in the summer between his junior and senior years, Bart Starr studied the game under the tutelage of the quarterback who led the Kentucky Wildcats to an upset victory over national champion Oklahoma in the Sugar Bowl. Starr later recalled that one of the most important lessons he learned was "huddle demeanor." Parilli, Starr said, "taught me how important it was to be the boss in the huddle and to communicate absolute confidence and focus to your teammates, because they will feed off that."[67] It was a lesson that served Bart Starr well throughout his college and NFL career.

Longtime NBA coach Pat Riley told me about his 1981 decision to leave the broadcast booth and take the job as head coach of the Los Angeles Lakers. Though he had enjoyed a successful playing career, Riley had no coaching experience. He was tackling a tough job which involved riding herd on such talented, strong-willed, temperamental athletes as Magic Johnson, Kareem Abdul-Jabbar, and James Worthy. He quickly found his authority being challenged by some of his players—and he began to doubt himself.

After one Monday practice, Lakers majority owner Jerry Buss approached him and said, "Pat, don't be afraid to coach the team." That's all he said—and all he needed to say. From then on, Pat Riley asserted his authority without a hint of self-doubt. He later told me, "That's the single-best piece of leadership advice I've ever gotten."

So step up, be bold, and be a leader on your team.

The Seventh Side of Leadership: A Serving Heart

Great leaders are role models of service to others. A profile of Coach Mike Krzyzewski in *Investor's Business Daily* tells of a basketball practice when a player handed a cup of water to the coach. The player let go of the cup before Krzyzewski had a good grip on it, and the cup fell and splashed water on the floor. A student assistant brought a towel from the equipment cart and was about to wipe up the spill.

"I'll take that," said Coach K—then he added, "When you are the CEO of your own company, I want you to remember that you should still clean up your own mess." Then he stooped down and mopped up the floor.[68] Leaders are servants to others. They don't demand to be served.

If you want to be the best teammate anybody has ever had, be a leader of vision, a leader who communicates, a leader who uses people skills and demonstrates character and competence, a leader who is bold, and above all, a leader who serves.

Leadership is influence. Your teammates are watching you, and you are leading them and influencing them by the way you live your life. Use your influence to impact your teammates in a positive way, and you'll be the Ultimate Teammate, guaranteed.

7 BE TEACHABLE
AND COACHABLE

"Be willing to be a beginner every single morning."

—Philosopher Meister Eckhart

Fuse/Thinkstock

Rob Sullivan is an assistant coach at St. Joseph's, and he was a sophomore basketball player there in 2003–2004, when Jameer Nelson was a senior. He recalls, "Jameer has an intense competitive nature, and he held all of us to a high standard of excellence for both our practices and games. Jameer also held himself to a high standard of excellence. Because he was humble, he was always teachable and coachable—and he expected nothing less from his teammates."

Great teammates are teachable and coachable. To be the Ultimate Teammate, be a sponge and soak up all you can. Coaches and teammates love having players on the team who are willing to learn and grow. A coachable player often becomes a player-coach, a mentor and teacher to the younger players.

Coachable players and coachable teams always go the farthest and achieve the highest heights. Years ago, when my son Bobby was a baseball player at Rollins College, I talked to a Major League scout about a young man who had been one of Bobby's teammates. I said, "I've heard great things about So-and-So. Where do you think he's going to be drafted?"

The scout hemmed and hawed and made some noncommittal sounds.

I said, "Hey, this kid is really talented. I've seen him play. I'd think some team would want to snatch him up pretty quick."

The scout shrugged and said, "Sure, he's got talent—but the word I get on the guy is that he's not coachable. He thinks he already knows it all, and his coaches can't tell him anything." And, as it turned out, that talented young player was drafted in a late round and had a short, lackluster career.

I have worked with some of the legendary coaches of the NBA—Jack Ramsay, Dick Motta, Cotton Fitzsimmons, Gene Shue, Billy Cunningham, Matt Guokas, Brian Hill, Doc Rivers, Stan Van Gundy, and more. Each one has had his own unique style and approach to the game, yet at one time or another I have heard of them ask much the same question about draft prospects: "Can I coach him? Will he listen? Is he teachable?"

And remember, this is at the NBA level, where many players come in thinking they've already learned it all. If being coachable is so important at the highest level of the game, it's vitally important at every other level, in every other endeavor in life.

The late baseball catcher and manager Johnny Oates once said, "Some players come up fast, but they waste their talents no matter what you do. They're just not coachable." In order for a team to be synchronized, unified, and successful, the players on the team must be coachable. If you don't have coachable players, you don't have a team. You just have a collection of flying egos.

A Sign of Strength

To be teachable and coachable is to be willing to accept instruction and correction—and willing to act affirmatively on that instruction and correction. A teachable, coachable teammate is willing to say, "I have a lot to learn," and even, "I was wrong." We can't become all we were meant to be without learning from others who are older, wiser, and more experienced. In order to reach our full potential, we must be taught and coached and brought to maturity in our character and our skills.

Former NBA coach Jack Ramsay gave me my first job in the NBA. When he took over as coach of the Portland Trail Blazers in 1976, his first order of business was to have a heart-to-heart talk with his star center, Bill Walton. He later recalled, "I met with Bill Walton to explain the game I wanted to play and his role in it. He seemed pleased with the theory, and yet I remember his comment as we finished our meeting: 'Coach, one last thing—don't assume we know anything.'"[69]

What did Bill Walton mean? He was telling Ramsay that he was teachable and coachable. He and his teammates wanted to learn all they could about playing basketball at the NBA level. Even after four years of playing for Coach John Wooden at UCLA, Bill Walton knew there was so much more he had to learn—so he told his new coach he and his teammates were ready to learn it. When Ramsay heard Bill Walton say those words, he was sure he'd have a great team—and he was right. That season, Jack Ramsay coached the Portland Trail Blazers to an NBA championship.

Soon after Phil Jackson took over as head coach of the Chicago Bulls, he called a meeting with Michael Jordan. Phil told Michael, "You've got to share the spotlight with your teammates."

"Well," Jordan said, "I think we're going to have trouble when the ball gets to certain people, because they can't pass and they can't make decisions with the ball."

"I understand that," Jackson said, "but I think if you give the system a chance, they'll learn to be playmakers. The important thing is to let everybody touch the ball so they won't feel like spectators. It's got to be a team effort."

"Okay," Michael Jordan said, "you know me. I've always been a coachable player. Whatever you want me to do, I'm behind you."

Phil Jackson recalled, "From then on, Michael devoted himself to learning the system and finding a way to make it work for him."[70]

Notice that a coachable player can still express opinions and reservations. A coachable player shouldn't argue with every instruction the coach gives, but it's certainly legitimate to raise an occasional concern with your coach. Ultimately, a coachable player must say, as Michael Jordan said to his coach, "I've always been a coachable player. Whatever you want me to do, I'll do it."

You probably know how miserable it can be to have an uncoachable teammate. An uncoachable teammate always says, "Why are you on my back? It wasn't my fault!" Or, "What are you yelling at me for? He was supposed to cover that one!" Or, "You should talk to those guys about that. I wasn't in position to make a play!" An uncoachable teammate never learns because he already knows it all. Nothing is ever his fault—so he'll probably try to pin the blame on you. He's always complaining that his coaches and teammates are unfair or stupid or incompetent. He blames his failures on the officials, the weather conditions, or the sun in his eyes, and he never takes responsibility for anything.

Whenever a coach or teammate tries to give him constructive advice, no matter how carefully stated, an uncoachable teammate is defensive, obnoxious, and argumentative. He refuses to listen to constructive advice—and he refuses to learn.

Uncoachable players usually have a higher opinion of their own skills than is warranted. This is because they take credit for their accomplishments and shift the blame for their failures. To them, accepting coaching from others is a sign of weakness. What uncoachable players don't understand is that their unwillingness to accept coaching is itself a sign of weakness. They mistakenly think that taking advice from others somehow makes them appear less capable. In fact, it is the person who is strong and secure in his own ego who is truly able to accept coaching and criticism. Being coachable is a sign of inner strength. The insecure, unteachable, uncoachable player is the one who truly looks weak and pathetic.

A mentally strong and emotionally secure player is eager to learn, listen, and apply coaching so he can step up his game. As Coach John Wooden once said, "It's what you learn after you know it all that counts." Great teammates never stop learning, never stop listening, and never reject coaching.

Listen—and Learn

Think back over your behavior in recent team settings. Have you been a coachable teammate? Or have you been a know-it-all? If, after careful self-examination, you have to confess that you have been an uncoachable teammate, let me offer you a little straight-from-the-shoulder coaching myself. Following are some suggestions for becoming a more teachable, coachable teammate:

Focus on listening.

The first step in learning is listening. There are many people around you—teammates, coaches, teachers, and others—who have experience and insight they can share with you. But in order to receive it, you have to be a good listener.

Ask questions.

Don't expect coaches and experienced teammates to volunteer the insights and information you need. Ask questions. People love to be asked, because it means that you value their experience and knowledge. When you ask people questions, you honor them and compliment them. And you'll be surprised at how much you will learn.

I am bullish on asking good questions. Whether I'm conducting a business meeting or chatting with strangers at the airport or interviewing celebrities on my radio shows, I want to ask good questions. People are fascinating, and we can learn so much from them, if we know how to draw them out. Great questions almost always begin with one of six key words: *what, where, when, how, why,* or *who.* When you ask a question beginning with one of those six words, the other person cannot answer with a simple yes or no, but must give you an answer that is thoughtful, informative, and interesting.

Asking good questions is an art form, and I've found that if you learn the skill of asking questions, the people you talk to—from presidents to sports stars to the guys who mop the floors at night—will say, "What a great question! And what a brilliant, insightful person you are!" Whenever you meet someone, put some thought and effort into the questions you ask that person. Asking questions is a tremendous skill, and anyone can learn and improve that skill.

Take advantage of teachable moments.

What is a teachable moment? It's any time a lesson presents itself to be learned. For example, when you make a mistake during practice or in a game, that is a teachable moment. Ask your coach or teammate, "What did I do wrong? What could I have done better? How would you have handled that situation?" Become a sponge for knowledge, especially at times when you make a mistake. Don't let any teachable moment go to waste.

Learn from experience.

You can learn a lot from experience, but experience can only teach you if you are teachable. If you blow it once, that's a mistake. If you blow it a second time exactly the same way, it's no longer a mistake—it's a choice. And it's a failure to learn from experience. Even coachable people make mistakes. But uncoachable people make the same mistake over and over again.

Treat mistakes as feedback, not failures.

Uncoachable people find it hard to admit mistakes because they view a mistake as a failure that diminishes them in their own eyes and the eyes of others. But coachable people find it easy to admit mistakes because they see mistakes as feedback, as information they can use to do better next time. To become a more coachable teammate, view your mistakes as useful information. Instead of saying, "I messed up.

I'm such a failure," try a more constructive approach: "Well, that didn't work. Oh well, I'll learn from it and try a different approach next time."

Have faith in your coach, and give up control.

Why is it important to have faith in your coach? Because you, as a player, don't always understand what your coach is trying to accomplish. You don't see the big picture; your coach does. Very often, when your coach tries to get you to try a new technique, skill, system, or strategy, things seem to get worse before they get better. You have to believe in your coach and surrender control in order to learn what your coach is trying to teach you. Stick with it, have faith, be coachable—and the benefits and results of that coaching will eventually become clear to you.

Deliberately and intentionally focus on being more teachable and coachable.

Every day, make a point of asking yourself, "Did I have a teachable attitude today? Was I a teachable and coachable teammate at practice today? Am I being a good listener? Am I open to new ideas and new ways of doing things? Am I willing to change my views and my methods based on new insight and information? Do I learn from experience? Am I asking questions? Am I being defensive?"

By making a point of searching ourselves and answering these questions every day, we will gradually become the kind of teachable, coachable teammate who every coach and player loves to have on his team. Being teachable and coachable is a key ingredient of being the best teammate anybody ever had.

Business writer August Turak recalls a time some years back when his golf game was in desperate shape. He turned for help to a golf pro who had PGA Tour experience. After his first months of lessons, the pro said to him, "Augie, I enjoy teaching you. No matter what I ask you to do, you give me 150 percent. You'd be amazed at how many guys pay me just to argue with me. They don't really want to change. They'd rather be right than good." After six months of lessons, August Turak had taken his game from the 110s to the low 80s.

Looking back over both his golf game and his business career, Turak concludes, "My proudest achievement is my coachability." He adds, "A proverb says that only stupid men learn from experience. Wise men learn from other people's experience."[71]

It's true. If you want to be wise, be teachable and coachable.

Celebrate as Teammates

In 1973, I left the Chicago Bulls organization and became the general manager of the Atlanta Hawks. The team was loaded with talent, had been an annual playoff contender for more than a decade, but had never quite reached its potential. The 1973–1974 season looked to be a very promising year.

But just a few games into my first season with the Hawks, the team began to unravel. When the Hawks lost 16 of their first 17 road games after New Year's Day, I went into a deep, dark depression. How could this be happening? We had so much talent, and we had a brilliant coach in Cotton Fitzsimmons. But the team didn't gel; the players couldn't fly in formation.

I watched Cotton try every trick in the book to psych his players up, but nothing worked. I talked to Cotton and asked him what was wrong. His answer, in a word: "Pete."

Pete Maravich was the team's marquee star, and arguably one of the greatest talents to ever dribble a basketball. When he was inducted into the Basketball Hall of Fame, he was hailed as "perhaps the greatest creative offensive talent in history." And John Havlicek once called him "the best ball-handler of all time." What's more, he was surrounded by some stellar players, including top-scoring guard Lou Hudson and center Walt Bellamy, who had been the NBA first overall draft pick out of Indiana University in 1960 and a future Hall of Famer. The Hawks should have dominated the league. Instead they embarrassed themselves, game after game.

And the reason was Pete Maravich. He was brilliant, talented, supremely confident—and totally uncoachable. He refused to play within Cotton Fitzsimmons' system. "Pistol Pete" would rather wow the crowd with amazing individual performances than win championships as part of an overall team effort. And though Coach Fitzsimmons was one of the most brilliant basketball strategists to ever coach the game, he could find no way to coax Pete Maravich to play within his system.

At the end of that season, I cut a deal to send Pete to the New Orleans Jazz, where he played for the better part of seven seasons. Waived by the Jazz because of a bad knee, he became a free agent and signed with the Boston Celtics, where he played his last season in the NBA. Any hopes Pete might have had for a championship ring were dashed when the Celtics were eliminated in the 1980 Eastern Conference finals by Julius Erving and the Philadelphia 76ers (by that time, I had left Atlanta and was the 76ers general manager).

Late in his career, Pete figured out that he'd made a costly mistake to have spent most of his NBA career as an uncoachable run-and-gun basketball star. He might have had one or more NBA championships under his belt with the Atlanta Hawks. By being uncoachable, Pete cheated his coach, his teammates, and himself out of a big chunk of sports history.

There's a postscript to the Pete Maravich story: After his retirement, Pete had a dramatic Christian conversion experience, and became quite zealous for his faith. He spoke to audiences all over the country, sharing his newfound faith. I was always thrilled to be in the presence of the new Pete Maravich, and often called him a "modern-day apostle Paul." The sports world was shocked in 1988 when Pete died of a heart attack while playing a pickup basketball game with broadcaster James Dobson of Focus on the Family. Before his death, Pete had an impact on hundreds of thousands of lives—an impact that has lasted to this day.

If Pete could talk to you, I think he would tell you that even though he made it into the Hall of Fame, he regrets that he never celebrated an NBA championship with his teammates. Ask any player with a championship ring on his finger which honor means more, an individual honor or a team championship, almost every one would tell you that the most satisfying achievement is the one you celebrate with your teammates.

The way you achieve a championship is by being teachable and coachable. If you want to be the best teammate anybody has ever had, set aside your ego, and get ready to listen and learn. The Ultimate Teammate is always eager to be taught, eager to be coached, and eager to help elevate his team to the highest levels.

8

HIT THE
BOOKS

"Being in school is the best place to be if you are an athlete because you can structure your own time."

—Distance Runner Frank Shorter

Ariel Duhon/iStock/Thinkstock

Jameer Nelson has been committed to self-improvement at least as far back as his high school years. At Chester High, he excelled in baseball, football, and basketball (though his baseball coach tried to get him to give up basketball, telling him he was too short to have a future in the NBA!).

But academics didn't come as easily to Jameer Nelson. In his early high school career, he was a D student. Not content to remain near the bottom of his class, Jameer asked a former Chester High student, Earl Pearsall, to be his tutor and mentor. With Earl's help, Jameer brought his D average up to college-qualifying Bs and Cs. Piersall also introduced Jameer to the St. Joseph's basketball coach, Phil Martelli. Arriving at St. Joe's, Jameer majored in sociology and excelled in basketball.

To this day, Jameer remains a strong supporter of education. He taped a public service announcement for the Orange County School Board's "Education Is Cool" campaign, and has even served as a school crossing guard at several Orlando schools. He wants young people to get the message that education is not only cool; it's the key that unlocks the door of the future.

If you want to be the best teammate anybody has ever had, then you've got to focus on your education. You've got to be a great scholar-athlete. Get the grades. Keep them up. Maintain your eligibility.

You can't be a good teammate if you're not eligible to play. If you flunk out, you've let everybody down, including your teammates. Your teammates are counting on you, not only on the field but in the classroom. The sport you play is over all too soon. You need to have goals far beyond your immediate athletic career. Begin reaching for those goals now.

So hit the books. Be a scholar-athlete your teammates can count on.

The Five Key Skills of Academic Success

You must master five key skills in order to achieve academic success. Unfortunately, many students—including all too many athletes—get all the way through high school and on into college without ever acquiring those five skills.

You may be one of those who never learned those skills. Maybe no one took the time to teach them to you, and you didn't even know you needed them. All you knew was that some people seem to have an easy time studying and getting grades, but for you it has always been a struggle.

The problem is not that you lack brains or intelligence. The problem is simply that no one has ever taught you how to study. In the next few pages, I'm going to give you a quick-start course in how to study. I'm going to show you how to acquire the five key skills you need in order to succeed in school. The five essential skills for academic success are:

1. Motivation
2. Organization
3. Time management
4. Focus
5. Taking notes

Let's look at each of these skills in order.

First Skill: Motivation

None of the other skills mean anything if you are not, first and foremost, motivated to succeed. Motivation is something you have to summon up from within yourself. Your academic success is tied to your athletic success. If you fail academically, you throw your athletic goals and dreams out the window.

Moreover, self-improvement—including intellectual and academic self-improvement—should be a major goal in your life. Your athletic career won't last forever. In fact, it probably won't last more than a few years. You have to look beyond your athletic career and think about the life you'll be living when you are no longer a student or professional athlete.

You have to want academic success for you and no one else. This isn't about pleasing your parents or your coaches or even your teammates. This is about looking out for Number One. You are far more than the sum of your athletic skills. You are more than just a "jock." You are a complete human being, and there's a whole wide world out there for you to explore. If you give education a chance, subjects like science, medicine, sociology, psychology, economics, foreign languages, history, art, literature, and music may just fascinate you. Start now to become a well-rounded human being with many interests beyond sports.

A friend of mine, writer Jerry Jenkins, has called me a "Renaissance jock," meaning that I am a sports fanatic who is also fascinated by history, biography, social science, politics, business, theology, and many other subjects. I have spent my entire career in the world of professional sports, yet I have also managed to read about 400 books per year. I have been committed to personal improvement, especially the improvement of my mind, throughout my life. I can't think of a better way to live. I encourage you to consider becoming a complete and well-rounded human being in body, mind, and spirit. Let that be your motivation to inspire you and carry you throughout your academic career.

When you achieve your goal of graduating from the university or college of your choice, when you have emerged as a complete and successful scholar-athlete, I hope you'll send me a note or email and let me know that you accepted this challenge. Let me know that you adopted this goal as your motivation, and that you reached your goal. If I get just one note from one scholar-athlete saying, "Pat, I did it! I graduated! I excelled! I maintained my motivation and my eligibility throughout my college career," I will know that this chapter was worth writing.

Second Skill: Organization

Getting organized is not all that hard, and an organized approach can make the rest of your academic life so much easier. When you are organized, you are able to keep track of your schedule, your assignments, and your study resources.

Begin by making a Things-to-Do list every day. Keep it in a place that you can easily access throughout the day, whether in a notebook or on your electronic tablet or phone. Put the most important tasks at the top of your list, and tackle them first. Don't put off important tasks for last, because you may not get to them at all. If you need a little extra motivation for tackling unpleasant tasks at the top of your list, promise yourself a reward—say, a fat-free latte or a half-hour with a good book—for getting those tasks finished.

As you carry out the tasks on your Things-to-Do list, be sure to check them off. Every time you complete a task and check it off your list, your brain experiences a little rush of endorphins, a sense of well-being that comes from getting things accomplished.

Another aspect of being organized is making sure you always have your school work with you. Do you have a reading assignment? A test to study for? A paper to write? Keep it with you on your laptop computer, tablet, or smart phone. That way, if you have some down time, you can use that time for reading, studying, or writing instead of letting those moments go to waste.

Plan ahead and make sure you're always ready, wherever you are, to make the best possible use of your time. A habit of being organized is a habit that will serve you well not only in school but throughout your adult life.

For nearly 25 years, my wife Ruth has been employed by the Franklin Covey Company. She teaches time management, organizational skills, project management, leadership, Stephen R. Covey's *The 7 Habits of Highly Effective People*® course, and a course on how to use your Franklin Planner. I carry my Franklin Planner with me everywhere I go (Franklin Covey also offers PlanPlus Online personal planner software for your computer, phone, or tablet). Ever since Ruth taught me how to use my Franklin Planner in 1995, I have never been without it.

I used to write my schedule and appointments on the back of used envelopes. Today, I have all of my day-by-day information logged and saved. I can go to my planner and tell you what I will be doing a year from now, or what I did at any given hour of any given day during the past two decades. I can tell you who I phoned, where I traveled, and even what I was thinking. Though you may never get to take one of Ruth's life-changing courses, you can become a more organized and prepared person. In the rest of this chapter, I'll give you a sampling of what it is like to learn under her tutelage.

Third Skill: Time Management

The key to academic success is using your time wisely. Most students who are never taught time management skills tend to put off projects and assignments until just before they're due. It's important that you learn to plan ahead and organize your time into productive blocks so that you can reduce stress, learn more effectively, and balance your life between academic work, athletics, and getting proper nutrition and rest.

Maintain a monthly calendar for scheduling your assignments. Write down the due dates for your papers and exams in your different classes. Work backward from those due dates to set goals for accomplishing large projects in stages. Break down each assignment into smaller tasks. For example, if you need to write a paper, set separate deadlines for doing your research, writing your first draft, and revising and writing your final draft. You can maintain this calendar in a paper notebook or on any electronic device you prefer.

When planning your daily schedule, find your most productive time of the day to work. Are you a morning person or a night person? Is it easier for you to get up early or stay up late? Always do your most important brainwork when you are mentally at your best.

Have set times for study and homework, and keep those times sacred. Put your phone away, and don't fritter away your time on video games, social networks, or texting. Save those activities for rewards when you get your work done. If your friends call you up and want you to go clubbing, partying, or just hanging out, say no. You can hang out some other night, after your work is done, but not during your study time. Don't let unmotivated people without any goals drag you down to their level. You are a scholar-athlete on a mission, and you refuse to leave your post until your mission is accomplished.

As you build good study habits, you will discover how long it takes to complete certain tasks, such as studying for a test or writing a paper. This knowledge will help you to schedule your activities on a weekly basis. Make sure you allow yourself enough time to get all your school work done. Also, make sure you schedule time for rest and relaxation. I don't want you to become a workaholic; I just want you to succeed.

It's important to do first things first, and tackle the chores and tasks on your schedule in order of priority. We have a tendency to put off important-but-intimidating chores until last. We prefer to start with the easy stuff, even if it is far less important than the difficult stuff.

Make a list of everything you need to get done, both your school work and non-school-related chores. Assign those chores a priority number from Priority 1 to Priority 3. Your Priority 1 tasks and activities are the most important. Make sure the chores related to your academic success are appropriately labeled Priority 1—and schedule your Priority 1 tasks and chores first. Always do first things first, so that when those Priority 1 tasks are done, you can enjoy your free time without stress, worry, or guilt.

Your list of priorities will evolve over time. Check your list frequently to make sure your most important tasks are being accomplished, your most important deadlines are being met, and that you are moving successfully toward your academic goals.

Fourth Skill: Focus

In order to meet your academic goals, you must be able to concentrate on your work. You must *focus*. We can't always screen out every distraction. A dorm room or your bedroom at home may not be the best environment for study. Find a place where you can study with limited interruption and distraction—the basement, a friend's house, or the library.

When I was a student at Wake Forest University, the library was my favorite spot to study. My dorm area was always rocking with loud music, shouting, and laughter. So, after baseball practice and dinner, I would usually get to the library by eight and stay until closing time at 11. I was far from a Phi Beta Kappa, but I did my best, and the library was a life-saver for me.

To do your best work at school, I suggest you turn off the TV, the phone, and the social media. If music helps you relax and focus, then listen to music. But avoid any and all temptations to waste time. Discipline yourself to put in a full 60 minutes of learning for every study hour on your schedule.

Do your studying in a clean, uncluttered environment. A cluttered desk leads to cluttered thinking. Keep your surroundings neat and orderly, because order is conducive to concentration.

Don't waste time on unimportant tasks. When you are in study mode, check your list of priorities and things to do, and focus on first things first. No procrastinating! If you need help with an assignment, get help from a teacher, professor, or tutor. But don't spin your wheels or waste time.

Every night, make sure you get a good night's sleep. Don't try to get by on Starbucks® or Red Bull®. Caffeine is no substitute for sleep. Your brain needs a certain number of hours of REM sleep every night in order to function at its peak. And the same brain you use for academic work is also a vital component of your athletic work. Your physical strength is in your muscles, but your quickness, game skills, and motor skills reside mostly in your brain. Whether as a scholar or an athlete, you need a high-functioning, alert brain in order to focus on the task at hand.

Don't strain your brain. Schedule adequate time for sleep.

Fifth Skill: Taking Notes

As you sit in class, you may be wondering why you have to spend the hour listening to your professor droning on and on. Well, hello! All of that "droning" is the information you're going to be tested on. That's important stuff. That's the point of the whole class.

Instead of holding your smart phone down in your lap, checking your texts and thinking (mistakenly) the professor doesn't know what you're doing, I suggest you start listening to that "droning" and taking good notes on it. It just might come in handy when it's time to regurgitate it on the exam.

What is the purpose of taking notes? Well-organized notes help you to key in on the most important ideas in the lecture—the ideas you need to know in order to get good grades. If you don't take good notes, you won't remember anything after you walk out of the classroom. Your instructor frequently dispenses information that won't be in your textbook, but will be on the test. This is your one and only chance to obtain that information. Don't blow it.

In the lecture, your instructor gives you clear indications as to what he thinks is important and what you will be tested on. The instructor also gives you your assignments in the lecture. So, by taking clear, accurate, well-organized notes, you greatly increase your chances of knowing what you need to know in order to get a good grade. With that in mind, following are some pointers for taking excellent notes:

- *Come prepared*, with all of your homework assignments and outside reading completed. Maintain an eager, open-minded, receptive attitude. You may not like your professor's personality, speaking style, or manner, but don't let that get in the way of your learning process and earning good grades. Listen carefully. Even if your professor seems dull, has an abrasive personality, or exhibits an annoying point of view, set all of that aside, and prepare yourself to learn.
- *Sit up front.* A front-row seat eliminates distractions and helps keep you focused on the reason you're there. Arrive on time—or better yet, arrive early—and get your note-taking materials ready (paper, pen or pencil, computer or tablet, and recorder).
- *Before class begins,* look over your previous notes, your course outline, and any other handouts or papers you may have received. Get your head into the game. Think about the subject of the class, the key topics, and the ideas the professor will be discussing. Think of questions to ask about the topics, and jot them down. Your questions will probably be answered by the lecture itself. If not, when the lecture is over, ask away!
- *Copy everything* the instructor writes on the blackboard, transparencies, or PowerPoint.
- *Listen carefully.* Be attentive to the lecture. Follow along in the outline. Learn to take brief notes, using abbreviations. Write legibly! Focus on jotting down key concepts and crucial information, not making a complete transcript of the instructor's words. Draw a box around assignments or assigned reading so you can spot them at a glance.

When the instructor indicates a main idea or key piece of information, underscore, star, or highlight that concept in your notes. Be alert to certain phrases your instructor uses to emphasize important points in the lecture: "First ..., second ..., third ..." "For example, ..." "This is important ... " "The key concept ... " "In conclusion, ... " "To sum it all up, ... " Your professor may have certain habitual phrases he uses to underscore an important point. Learn those phrases, and be alert to them at all times. Those phrases indicate material you can expect to encounter on the test.

After the lecture, ask questions about anything you don't understand. If necessary, stay after class to ask your questions.

Don't rush the learning process. Don't try to multitask during the lecture. Shut off your phone, put away anything that might be a distraction, and don't start gathering up your belongings until the lecture comes to a full and complete stop.

- *After the lecture,* take time to tidy up your notes. Make sure you go over your notes while your memory of the lecture is still fresh. Review your notes at least a couple of times before your next class, and make sure you have all the concepts and information clear in your mind.

- *Keep your notes safe and well-organized.* Keep separate files or notebooks for each course. If you take notes on paper, write on only one side of the page. If you keep your notes on a computer or tablet, back up your files at a secure location—in the "cloud" or on a separate hard drive—in case your device gets lost or stolen.

The more you practice note-taking, the more skilled you will become. You may find you can improve your athletic performance by taking notes on your coach's lectures. Like most skills we acquire in life, the skill of taking clear, concise notes in the classroom is a skill that can be transferred to many other arenas of life.

Motivation, organization, time management, focus, and taking notes are the five key skills of academic success. Master those skills and you can master your academic life—and you'll be well on your way to becoming the most academically well-rounded teammate anybody has ever had.

The 10 Commandments of Test-Taking

Finally, let's take a brief look at the skill of test-taking. Permit me to offer 10 suggestions—no, let's make that 10 *commandments*—for taking tests in school:

- *Commandment 1: Thou shalt not cram for thy test.* Schedule plenty of study time throughout the days leading up to the test. Know the material thoroughly—don't try to stuff it all into your brain the night before.

- *Commandment 2: Thou shalt not pull an all-nighter.* Your brain performs best when it has had adequate sleep.

- *Commandment 3: Thou shalt not skip breakfast before a test.* Good nutrition is crucial to effective brain performance.

- *Commandment 4: Thou shalt not show up late for thy test.* Don't just be on time; be early. Being relaxed and focused instead of stressed and frustrated can significantly improve your test performance.

- *Commandment 5: Thou shalt not get bogged down.* If you don't know the answer to a question, skip it and come back to it later (if you have time). Focus on answering the questions you know first. Monitor your time, and make sure you allow yourself enough time to finish the test.
- *Commandment 6: Thou shalt not second-guess thyself.* If you must guess on multiple-choice tests, go with your instinctive answer upon your first reading of the question. Pondering too long often leads test-takers to turn an initially correct answer into a wrong answer.
- *Commandment 7: Thou shalt not rush through the test to get out early.* Read questions carefully and make sure you understand them before marking your answer. At the end of the test, if you have time remaining, go back and recheck your answers. Try to answer questions you skipped. Put the entire test period to productive use.
- *Commandment 8: Thou shalt not turn in an unchecked exam paper.* This is no time to get careless. Take time to check your answers. If it's an essay test, make sure you proofread what you have written.
- *Commandment 9: Thou shalt not turn in an anonymous exam paper.* You'd be surprised how often test papers are turned in without the student's name at the top. Don't waste all your study and effort over such a simple mistake.
- *Commandment 10: Thou shalt not think negative thoughts.* Be positive and confident. You have every right to be confident because you have taken good notes, you have studied thoroughly, you have mastered the material, and you're going to do brilliantly.

You have your assignment. Master the five key skills of academic success: Get motivated. Get organized. Manage your time well. Stay focused. Take good notes. Then obey The 10 Commandments of Test-Taking. Hit the books, and become a great scholar-athlete. I know you can do it.

And when you get those good grades and maintain your academic eligibility, you'll be the best teammate anybody ever had.

9

BE FULLY
PREPARED

"The man who is prepared has his battle half-fought."

—Author Miguel de Cervantes

Ingram Publishing/Thinkstock

Jameer Nelson has always been obsessed with being fully prepared. Why does he bring his Magic teammates to Philadelphia in the off-season for a time of practice, instruction, team bonding, and relaxation? He does it to prepare himself and his teammates to fight their way through another NBA season.

Even when Jameer was a college player at St. Joseph's, he was a fanatic about preparation. His college basketball coach, Phil Martelli, recalled that it was Jameer who truly set the emotional tone for his teammates, both in practices and in the games. During practices, Jameer and his teammates liked to create a rhythm, punctuated by clapping and good-natured trash talk, as they went through their drills and plays. These rhythms carried over into the games, which Jameer and his teammates played with business-like, almost unemotional focus. They never celebrated or high-fived each other during the games. They just stayed in that rhythm and won game after game.

To be the best teammate anybody ever had, you have to be obsessed with preparation. You have to keep yourself in top shape, get the rest you need, get the good nutrition you need, and maintain your skills and physical conditioning even in the off-season. And you have to encourage your teammates to maintain their preparation as well.

Every player has to know the game plan backward and forward, inside and out. Every player has to be physically strong, mentally agile, and at the top of his skills. As racecar driver Bobby Unser once said, "Success is where preparation and opportunity meet." So heed the example of Jameer Nelson. When opportunity comes your way, make sure you're prepared for success.

Intensely Committed to Preparation

One of the most important ways we prepare ourselves is by maintaining our physical health, strength, endurance, and conditioning. We're not going to be much use to our teammates if we are dragging around like sleep-deprived zombies or laid up in the hospital because we've been neglecting our health and nutrition.

Any doctor will tell you that you need to get up and walk at least 10,000 steps a day, consume plenty of protein and whole grains, cut your intake of sugar, fat, and processed foods, stay hydrated, and avoid alcohol and tobacco. Daily low-impact exercise helps build bone and muscle mass, slims your mid-section, is great for your back, helps balance your hormones and regulate sleep patterns, increases your tolerance for pain and exertion, helps you feel better and think more clearly, keeps you young longer, and improves your ability to cope with stress.

The better shape you're in, the more valuable you are to your teammates. You owe it to them to maintain your peak physical performance.

My writing partner, Jim Denney, once conducted an in-depth interview with the legendary NFL defensive lineman Reggie White, who died as the result of a lung ailment in late 2004. Jim interviewed Reggie in Knoxville, Tennessee, in the spring of 1996, just months before Reggie collected an NFL Championship ring in Super Bowl XXXI. Jim told me:

> One of the most impressive traits of Reggie White was his commitment to preparation, including a commitment to staying in top condition, even in the off-season. During my visit to his home, he showed me his private workout room. Walking past his Olympic-size indoor pool, you come to a room filled with Reggie White-trademarked weight and exercise machines and a top-of-the-line Stairmaster. He turned on a CD by Take 6, got up on the Stairmaster, cranked it up to maximum resistance, and put himself through a workout that left him drenched in sweat. I felt the floor shaking underneath me as he exercised.
>
> Training camp was weeks away, yet Reggie worked out daily and kept himself in fighting trim. He told me that a lot of NFL players goof off in the off-season and report to training camp with a lot of extra pounds around the middle. But Reggie was committed to being the best, and he was willing to pay that price every day.
>
> Millions of people watched Reggie White, the finished product, competing on the football field. But I got to see something few people ever get to see. I got to see the product under construction. I saw Reggie White in the workout room, straining to be the best.
>
> He told me his commitment to staying in shape year-round went back to when he was at the University of Tennessee and he wanted to win Player of the Year in the SEC. He said, "I wanted to be the best, but I wasn't focused on the conditioning and training that would get me to those goals. So I got injured a lot in my junior year at U.T."
>
> Reggie compared the human body to a cable. He said, "Which is harder to break—a cable made of spaghetti or a cable made of steel? I wasn't working out like I should. So I got a sprung ankle in a game against Duke, and I sprung the other ankle in a game against Alabama. Then I got an elbow injury and a pinched nerve in my neck. The sports writers started saying that I wasn't tough enough for football."
>
> Reggie realized he needed to spend more time in the weight room. He told me that in his senior year, he did more weight training, more sprinting to build his speed, and more laps to build his endurance. As a result of his extra work, his game improved and he had fewer injuries.
>
> Soon after he began playing in the NFL, Reggie saw the Redskins-Giants game where Redskins quarterback Joe Theismann suffered a

career-ending broken leg. Reggie told me, "I saw that, and I knew I needed to armor-plate my body with muscle in order to have a long career in the league. In my rookie year with the NFL, I made up my mind I was going to be in better shape than anybody else."

Reggie had an infectious enthusiasm about him that spread to the entire team. His teammates on the Green Bay Packers—Brett Favre, Sean Jones, Santana Dotson, Keith Jackson, and the rest—all said that Reggie elevated the level of commitment of every player on the team. That's what a great teammate does—he spreads a contagious desire for winning to everyone. The Packers were healthier, better conditioned, more fired up and committed because of Reggie's influence. And less than a year after I met with Reggie in Knoxville, he and his teammates were all wearing Super Bowl rings.

Reggie White was on fire to be the best prepared, most physically conditioned player in the NFL. His passion for preparation set all his teammates on fire with that same passion. How about you? Are you intensely committed to being the best prepared player around? If you were as intense about preparation as Reggie White, what effect would it have on your teammates?

Preparation: The Key to Confident Performance

How important is preparation? Baseball great Hank Aaron told the graduating class of the Emory University School of Law, "In playing baseball, or in life, a person occasionally gets the opportunity to do something great. When that time comes, only two things matter: being prepared to seize the moment and having the courage to take your best swing."[72]

Bobby Bowden, who coached the Florida State Seminoles football team from 1976 to 2009, holds the NCAA Division I record for most career wins. For Bobby, preparation was the key to winning. He once told me that he and his staff spent one hour planning and preparing their game plan for every minute their players would be on the field. Their intense commitment to preparation showed.

Preparation is the key to confidence, and confidence is the key to functioning well under pressure and adversity. By preparing thoroughly in practice, you become confident to face any contingency in real life situations. No matter what happens, you are able to face it and say, "I've been here before. I can handle this."

I once heard retired Celtics forward Larry Bird talk about the importance of preparation in a TV interview. He said:

> I have to keep preparing myself to play, even in the off-season. I have to keep challenging myself to be ready. One of our guys came to training camp saying, "I didn't touch a basketball all summer." I said, "What did you do instead?" He said, "I lifted weights, I did yoga,

that sort of thing." I couldn't believe it. I thought, "How in the heck can a basketball player go all summer and not touch a basketball?" I couldn't do that. I had to be playing, shooting, practicing, and preparing. Even when I travel, I always have a basketball handy. If I didn't touch a basketball for one day, I'd feel I hadn't accomplished anything.

Among the best-prepared teams in sports history were the UCLA basketball teams coached by John Wooden. His practice sessions were efficient, up-tempo workouts that never wasted time or energy. His players were fully engaged in learning their assignments and sharpening their skills from the first whistle to the last.

Few of his players realized that those quick, economical practice sessions were the result of meticulous daily planning by Coach Wooden. He planned his sessions right down to the specific words he intended to use to motivate his players. Coach Wooden actually enjoyed the teaching process in the practices more than he enjoyed winning games. He said he missed the preparation of the practice sessions most when he retired. Coach Wooden recalled:

> I felt that running a practice session was almost like teaching an English class in that I wanted to have a lesson plan. I knew the detailed plan was necessary in teaching English, but it took a while before I understood the same thing was necessary in sports. Otherwise you waste an enormous amount of time, effort, and talent.
>
> I would spend almost as much time planning a practice as conducting it. Everything was listed on three-by-five cards down to the last detail. Everything was planned out each day. In fact, in my later years at UCLA I would spend two hours every morning with my assistants organizing that day's practice (even though the practice itself might be less than two hours long).[73]

Coach Wooden learned the importance of planning and preparation from his early days as a teacher and coach at South Bend Central High School in Indiana. While at South Bend, he befriended Notre Dame football coach Frank Leahy, and Leahy invited him to a Notre Dame practice. Coach Wooden watched Leahy take his players quickly from drill to drill with the trill of a whistle. Practices were not long, but efficiently organized and fast-paced. Coach Wooden recalled those lessons, and built them into his own practices, as he explained:

> There wasn't one second in the whole practice when anybody was standing around wondering what would come next. ... The whole thing was synchronized; each hour offered up sixty minutes, and I squeezed every second out of every minute.
>
> Players felt, at times, that the actual game against an opponent was slower than our practice in the gym. That's exactly the way I designed it.[74]

Coach John Wooden prepared his players by teaching them to execute plays with precision—and without thought or hesitation. Preparation is the key to confident, competent performance.

Preparing for Failure Produces Success

Coach Wooden believed that one of the most important ways to prepare for success is by preparing for failure. He once wrote:

> Failing to prepare is preparing to fail. … Failing to prepare for failure can prevent success. …
>
> A basketball team that has a pretty good night will miss 30 percent of its shots. That's a high rate of failure. Consequently, I instructed our players, "Assume every shot will be missed."
>
> I taught them to expect failure—the missed basket—and to be ready to do what comes next: a tip-in, rebound, fast break, or something else. "Don't just stand around waiting to see if the ball goes in. Assume it won't; get ready to respond quickly and correctly." … What happens after a missed opportunity, mistake, or failure is crucial. Perfection is impossible. Capitalizing on imperfection—mistakes—makes all the difference.
>
> Those I coached didn't need to visualize success. Success would take care of itself if they took care of everything else. This included preparing for failure.[75]

Bill Walton, Coach Wooden's star center in the early 1970s, recalled, "Practices at UCLA were nonstop, electric, supercharged, intense, demanding … with Coach pacing the sidelines like a caged tiger, barking instructions, positive reinforcement, and maxims: 'Be quick, but don't hurry.' He constantly changed drills and scrimmages, exhorting us to 'move quickly, hurry up.' Games seemed like they happened in a slower gear. I'd think in games, 'why is this taking so long,' because everything we did in games happened faster in practice."[76] And Swen Nater, who also played for Coach Wooden in the early 1970s, recalled:

> Coach Wooden's practice sessions were planned to the minute. Every activity lasted a predetermined amount of time, and time was never compromised, for any activity or for the duration of the session. Not a moment was wasted. When the whistle blew, signaling the end of a drill, players, coaches, and managers moved purposefully and quickly to the next drill in a machine-like manner. But there was quickness, not hurrying. Even before we were in place for the next activity, Coach was already shouting instructions. Seniors and experienced team members echoed his instructions to the rest of us. Efficiency, intensity, industriousness, and purpose dominated and controlled our effort and concentration.

He never let up. From the beginning to the end of practice, Coach commanded, exhorted, and demanded our best. He moved with us, around us, before us, and paced, stopped, and started, always setting the pace of practice and constantly increasing the tempo. Although off the court he was a mild-mannered man, when he stepped into his basketball classroom, he was an intense, very verbal, and possessed teacher who had three things on his mind—improvement, improvement, improvement. Off the court, that meant planning, planning, planning.[77]

If you want to be the best teammate anybody has ever had, adopt the mindset of the greatest coach of all time. Heed the example of Coach John Wooden, and make preparation your goal. And while you're at it, heed the example of Jameer Nelson, Reggie White, Hank Aaron, Bobby Bowden, and Larry Bird.

Prepare yourself mentally and physically. Prepare yourself strategically. Elevate the preparedness of your teammates through your enthusiasm, intensity, and good example. Prepare yourself to respond to mistakes and failures.

Then, prepare yourself for a lifetime of victories and successes.

10

COMMITTED

"When you work together with teammates, you can do remarkable things. If you work alone, you leave a lot of victories on the table. Collaboration has a multiplying effect on everything you do because it releases and harnesses not only your skills but also those of everyone on the team."

Pat Carroll, one of Jameer Nelson's teammates at St. Joe's, remembers Jameer as a player who was intensely committed to his team and to each of his teammates. He told me, "I always felt Jameer valued the success of the team as much as he did his own success.

And Coach Phil Martelli told me:

> We had a terrific team in the 2004. Jameer was back for his senior season and he led us to the highest heights. At the end of the season, he just missed a jump shot against Oklahoma State that would have sent us to the Final Four. At the press conference after the game, a reporter asked Jameer if coming back for his senior year had fulfilled all his goals for the season. Jameer said, "I came back to be the best teammate these guys ever had." That's a statement of Jameer's total commitment to his teammates. That's who Jameer is.

To be the best teammate anybody has ever had, be totally committed to your fellow players, to your team, to excellence, to competing hard, and to winning. If that is your commitment, you'll be the Ultimate Teammate, guaranteed.

Committed to Each Other

In his book *Why Teams Win*, Saul L. Miller talks about that indefinable dimension of teamwork we call "chemistry." And chemistry, he says, arises when teammates are committed to each other in an intense and meaningful way:

> Chemistry is the mortar that binds the bricks together.
>
> Chemistry is a feeling. That feeling evolves in the shared commitment people have performing and competing alongside each other in meaningful pursuits.
>
> Chemistry is feeling a part of the solution. It is expressed in respect for teammates and what each contributes. Chemistry is about everyone contributing. Winning chemistry occurs when the "we" is bigger and more important than "me." Winning chemistry is about selflessness, sacrifice, and support. Winning teams have chemistry.[78]

What does it mean to be totally committed to your teammates? Coach Vince Lombardi expressed the concept in a single word: *love*. He said, "When those tough sportswriters asked me what made the Packers click, I said, 'Love.' It was the kind [of love] that means loyalty, teamwork, respecting the dignity of another—heart power, not hate power."[79]

Bart Starr quarterbacked the Green Bay Packers during the Lombardi years, and he agreed that love was the key to the Packers' championship seasons. Starr recalls, "I personally believe attitude and love [were] two of the strongest words in our vocabulary."[80] To Starr, love means teamwork, camaraderie, mutual encouragement, and unity. And the versatile Paul Hornung, who played halfback, quarterback, and placekicker on Lombardi's Packers, recalled, "There was a genuine love on that football team, and I was glad to be a part of it."[81]

While I was general manager of the Philadelphia 76ers, I got to know third baseman Mike Schmidt, who played his entire career with the Phillies. In fact, we named our third son after Mike. I once heard Mike share his philosophy of teamwork, which he expressed in the phrase, "Share the love." Schmidt said:

> What does love have to do with winning baseball games? Well, love is the most powerful motivator there is. I'm not talking about love as an emotion, but love as an unconditional commitment to each other on the team. When a team develops that indefinable quality called "chemistry," it's because love is in the air. Players feel liberated to take risks and achieve great things because they know their teammates will support them and uphold them whether the ball bounces their way or not. They know their teammates are pulling for them no matter what, because the team is built on a foundation of love.

We talked about unconditional love, what the ancient Greeks called *agape*-love, in Chapter 6. But the subject bears repeating. Unconditional love, teamwork love, means that you unconditionally accept one another, support one another, affirm one another, and forgive one another even if your teammates disappoint you, and even if they are not all that lovable. You can love them even if you don't like them. In fact, that's when your teammates need your love the most—when they are at their unlikable worst. Unconditional love can hold the team together and unite teammates into an unbeatable force, in spite of personality differences, cultural differences, and all the other differences that threaten to divide you.

One of the most famous examples of a team bonded by love was the 1960 Philadelphia Eagles. In their first postseason appearance since 1949, the 1960 Eagles posted a season record of 10-2-0, and defeated the Green Bay Packers to win the NFL championship. Bill Campbell, the voice of Philadelphia sports in that era, later recalled that those players "got the most out of their ability and played way over their heads, no doubt about it. I've never seen a team that had so much camaraderie. Those guys really loved each other. They fought … among themselves sometimes, but at the same time they loved each other. … They weren't the best team in the league and weren't the best in their own division. But they were the best every Sunday."[82]

Retired Florida State Seminoles football coach Bobby Bowden explained it this way: "We talk about teams having chemistry: 'Man, this ball club had good chemistry.' I think what that means, you've got a bunch of boys that love and care for each other. You see, when somebody loves somebody, they'll fight for them; when somebody loves somebody, they'll defend them; when somebody loves somebody, they're not gonna let somebody hurt that person, and that's a big thing in football."[83]

Love for your teammates is a much stronger motivator than hatred for your opponent. If you want to have a championship team, respect your opponents and love one another. How do you show love to your teammates? By caring about their needs. By taking an interest in what's going on in their lives. By supporting them through the tough times. By celebrating with them in the good times. By overlooking their faults and flaws, just as you hope they'll overlook yours. By forgiving them for their failures. By lifting them up when they're down. By maintaining team unity, even when there is conflict and a clash of personalities.

Love is the glue that holds teams together. Be committed to loving your teammates, and you'll truly be a *team*—and a force to be reckoned with.

Committed to Healthy Friendships

Dwight Gooden was one of the most feared pitchers in the National League during the 1980s, yet rumors of drug abuse swirled around him for several years. After Gooden tested positive for cocaine during 1987 spring training, he entered drug rehab to avoid being suspended.

"Why did I do it? Because I was stupid," Gooden once told reporters. "My friends would say, 'Here, try it.' And I didn't have the strength to say no. I was too worried about what my friends would think of me if I said no."[84]

Dwight Gooden is just one of many professional athletes to succumb to the influence of unhealthy friendships. Running back Sammie Smith was selected by the Miami Dolphins in the first round of the 1989 NFL Draft after a legendary career at Florida State University. He played in the NFL from 1989 to 1992. In 1996, he was convicted of possession and distribution of cocaine, spending seven years in prison. Why did Sammie Smith get caught selling drugs to undercover officers?

"The only answer I can come up with," he told a reporter, "is stupidity. I didn't need money. I was fine."

At the time of his arrest, he was living off the remainder of a $2.5 million football contract and a half-million-dollar insurance settlement. He also had investments, real estate, cars, and a construction company. He didn't need to get involved with drugs. But like Dwight Gooden, Smith couldn't resist the corrupting influence of unhealthy friendships.

"It was a matter of hanging around these guys," Smith said. "These were my friends, and I just couldn't turn my back on them. We saw an easy way to make money."[85]

There's good news on the Sammie Smith story. He's gotten his life straightened out and works fulltime for the Fellowship of Christian Athletes in central Florida. The FCA has its offices in the same building that is home to the Orlando Magic, and I get to see Sammie frequently. He is having a great impact among young athletes in central Florida.

To be the best teammate anybody ever had, you must be committed to maintaining healthy friendships and severing unhealthy friendships that will only drag you down.

Retired NBA point guard Avery Johnson went on to coach two NBA teams—the Dallas Mavericks and New Jersey Nets. In his book *Aspire Higher*, Johnson warns about the influence of unhealthy friendships. He writes: "Begin by asking yourself these questions: With this person in my life, am I winning or losing? What sorts of things are they saying to me? The answer to the second question will help you answer the first one. What the people closest to you are saying to you every day has a profound effect on your state of mind and, in effect, your success."[86]

And Coach John Wooden affirms the importance of healthy friendships with our teammates—and the danger of unhealthy friendships. He writes:

> If we are going to successfully work with others, it is vital to know the function of friendship. After all, God created us to be dependent upon each other.
>
> Friendship comes from mutual esteem and devotion. Friendship is doing for others while they are doing for us. … Friendship goes both ways. … Friends help each other; they don't use each other. …
>
> Friends help to complete us, and we'll be better for having taken them along on our journey to becoming all we are capable of becoming.[87]

To be the best teammate anybody ever had, be committed to maintaining strong, healthy friendships with your teammates. Remove yourself from any so-called "friendships" with people who will only bring you down. Don't let unhealthy "friends" who don't really care about you destroy your self-worth, your future, and your value to your teammates.

Committed to Excellence and Winning

Bill Curry, former head football coach at Georgia Tech, Alabama, Kentucky, and Georgia State, played on four NFL teams. He looks back fondly on his years playing center with quarterback Johnny Unitas on the Baltimore Colts, 1967 through 1972. Curry remembers his legendary teammate as a man who was intensely committed to excellence and to winning.

> In downtown Baltimore … there is a huge statue of John Unitas. I stopped by recently to get a solo look. … I hung around for a while, deeply saddened by the fact that John had died on September 11th, 2002, just a month before the dedication date on the pedestal. As I turned to leave, I took one more backward glance, looked up, and into the eyes. I had looked directly into those eyes across a huddle for five campaigns. Those eyes always told me one thing: "We are going to win." …

He loved every tiny, obscure, mundane detail of the game he played at the highest level. … He was the only football player I have ever known who loved, even craved, every sordid detail of our existence. I swear to you, he even seemed to like the pain. At the very least, he didn't let it distract him from the business at hand: finding a way to win. …

If you go there to visit the historic statue—and I know that I will return—be sure to look into his eyes.

They are the eyes of a winner.[88]

Bill Curry remembers Johnny Unitas as the best teammate he ever had. Why? Because Unitas was intensely committed to winning.

Former New York Giants general manager Ernie Accorsi spent more than a decade working with the Baltimore Colts. Ernie told me that Johnny Unitas was the greatest example of leadership under pressure he ever knew. Unitas projected an air of quiet confidence whenever the Colts were on the road. When the team bus arrived at the opposing team's stadium, the fans from that city would often surround the bus, yelling insults at the players and rocking the bus, trying to intimidate Unitas and the Colts. But Johnny would stand up, walk down the center aisle, and step off the bus, right in the teeth of the hostile crowd. Johnny had such a commanding presence that the opposing fans would part in front of him like the Red Sea parting before Moses. Unitas would lead his team into the facility—and his teammates knew that everything was going to be okay.

I once spoke at a convention, and I heard one of my fellow convention speakers tell a story about playing a board game with his 11-year-old son. They had played the game 11 times, and the dad had won all 11 games. After each game, his son had said, "Just one more game." The dad had agreed again and again, but it was getting late, and he was getting tired of the game. So he told his son, "Not tonight. It's time for bed."

"Daddy," the boy said, "I can't go to bed yet. We have to play another game."

"But son, it's already past your bedtime."

"Daddy, you don't understand. We can't stop playing until I win."

Then the father understood—and he agreed to a 12th game. This time, the boy won. We can all learn a lesson from that 11-year-old boy. He was intensely committed to winning. Is your commitment to winning as intense as his?

Retired Celtics star Larry Bird understood the absolute compulsion to win—and that's what made him such a great teammate. He once said, "I think when guys make the commitments sometimes, maybe their hearts weren't in it. I don't know, I can't speak for 'em. My heart's in this. I want to win. I crave winning."[89] How about you? Are you so committed to winning that you actually *crave* winning?

Nobody goes undefeated all the time. But winners have a grudge against losing. To people who are committed to winning, losing leaves a bad taste in the mouth. Losing is painful, almost intolerable. And when you lose, your first thought is figuring out why you lost and how to keep from losing next time.

If you are committed to winning, nothing feels worse than being on a team with teammates who are easy-going about losing. People who are committed to winning can't understand anyone who isn't. We who crave winning know that life is competition. Though we prize good sportsmanship, we know there's no prize for those who are "good losers." We don't respect cheating, we refuse to win at the cost of our integrity, but we are willing to pay any price, make any sacrifice, in order to win honorably. We are committed to getting the most out of our ability. We hate the idea of losing so much that will do almost anything to win.

As Coach Vince Lombardi once put it, "I firmly believe that any man's finest hour is that moment when he has worked his heart out in a good cause and lies exhausted on the field of battle, victorious." That is what we crave. That is what we are committed to. There are certain qualities that characterize all winners:

- *Winners are committed to teamwork.* Winners prize a team achievement over individual accomplishments. A winner always wants to be a great teammate to others, and wants to be part of a great team.
- *Winners are committed to learning and growth.* A winner doesn't assume he already knows it all, but is always hungry to learn more. Winners hold themselves to high standards of continuous growth and self-improvement.
- *Winners have stick-to-it-ivity.* There's no quit in them. They may go down in defeat, but they never, ever surrender. Right up until that final buzzer sounds, they are continually, tenaciously looking for a way to win.
- *Winners are cheerleaders for their teammates.* They praise, empower, and motivate. They build up their teammates, never tear them down. They celebrate their teammate's successes. When their teammates fail, they say, "Chin up, we'll get 'em next time!"
- *Winners keep their commitments.* They honor their word. They show up on time. They work hard in practice. They fight hard in games. They never let their coaches or teammates down. Winners demonstrate their commitment through their actions.

One of the most committed competitors I've ever met was baseball pitcher Bob Feller, who played 18 seasons for the Cleveland Indians. He pitched from 1936 to 1941, did a four-year hitch in the Navy during World War II, and then pitched again from 1945 to 1956. In his long career, Bob Feller posted a record of 266 wins (including 44 shutouts) and 162 losses.

I got to talk to Bob Feller in 2000, when he was 81 years old. We were at an event honoring Ted Williams. I knew that Bob had just turned 23 when Pearl Harbor was attacked on December 7, 1941. Two days after the attack, Bob joined the Navy and went to war. At the time he left baseball to join the Navy, Bob had been leading the American League in strikeouts for four straight years, yet he didn't hesitate for a moment to sacrifice his career in order to serve his country. I asked Bob why he joined so quickly and didn't try to remain in baseball as long as possible.

"We were at war," Bob said firmly, "and we were losing. I hate to lose. I had no choice but to go and fight."

Whether on the pitcher's mound in the States or in a gun turret aboard USS Alabama, Bob Feller hated to lose—and he was intensely committed to winning. In fact, even while he was in the Navy, he would keep his pitching arm in shape by throwing baseballs to his fellow sailors on the deck. Serving on ships in both the north Atlantic and the Pacific theater of operations, Bob Feller saw plenty of combat, and he left the service with decorations that included six campaign ribbons and eight battle stars.

How about you? Are you intensely committed to excellence and to winning? How much do you hate to lose? How much do you love to win?

If you want to be the best teammate anybody ever had, you must be intensely committed to your fellow teammates, to healthy friendships, and to winning, winning, winning. Total commitment is essential to being the Ultimate Teammate.

DON'T
QUIT

"Perseverance—secret of all triumphs"

An NBA season consists of 82 games—41 at home and 41 away. I've been working in the NBA since 1968, so I have seen literally thousands of basketball games over my career. Most of them, understandably, blend together in my memory, but a few games stand out quite vividly. One particularly memorable game was a Magic home game against the Denver Nuggets on March 18, 2011.

The Magic led throughout much of the game, but in the final quarter, our guys had the cold hand. They repeatedly turned the ball over, struggled at the free throw line, and made only a third of their shots from the field. The Nuggets patiently chipped away at our lead. Finally, with 5.7 seconds remaining, the Nuggets tied the game at 82.

How many times over the years had I seen a team squander a big lead, and finally lose at the buzzer or in overtime? Too many to count. I had a bad feeling about this game.

The ball was inbounded to Jameer, who dribbled away the final seconds near the top of the key. The hometown crowd was thinking exactly what I was thinking: *Shoot it, Jameer! Shoot!*

Jameer jumped and released a shot that barely cleared the extended fingertips of Nuggets defender Ty Lawson. The buzzer sounded as the ball was in mid-arc. The crowd held its breath. The ball fell—

A perfect swish for three beautiful points.

The Magic had struggled to hang on throughout the fourth quarter—and our guys' perseverance had paid off at the final buzzer. I later heard Magic reserve guard Quentin Richardson, who played 21 minutes that night, sum up the lessons of that game for a reporter: "When bad things happen and you're plagued by adversity," he said, "you've just got to persevere and grind it out or pull it out, no matter how you get it."

That's what Jameer Nelson and his Magic teammates did that night. They struggled, but they persevered. They got the win any way they could get it, even in the teeth of adversity.

When you and your teammates feel the momentum shifting against you, when you feel the game slipping away from you, don't quit. Persevere. Keep fighting. Pull out the win any way you can.

To be the best teammate anybody ever had, be a teammate who refuses to quit. Be a teammate who inspires the entire team to persevere.

A Teammate Who Refuses to Quit

Quitters don't win, and winners don't quit. A great example of a winner who wouldn't quit is retired NFL defensive end Jack Youngblood, who played for the Los Angeles Rams from 1971 to 1984. Youngblood only missed one game in his NFL career, and he holds the franchise record for consecutive games played, 201.

On December 30, 1979, Jack Youngblood and the Rams played the Dallas Cowboys in the divisional championship game. Late in the first half, Youngblood got chop blocked by a pair of Dallas offensive linemen. He felt something snap, then he went to the ground, grimacing in pain. The trainers carted him into the locker room for x-rays. The pictures showed that Youngblood had a broken fibula—a snapped calf-bone. The break was just above the ankle.

The doctor told him he was done for the day. Youngblood wouldn't hear it. "Tape up my leg," he replied, "and bring me some aspirin."

The doctor showed him the x-ray. "Look. Your fibula's snapped like a pencil!"

Youngblood growled, "It's my leg and my career!"

The doctor taped up his leg, but he warned Youngblood that there wasn't a painkiller that would numb a broken bone. Youngblood shrugged, got to his feet, and walked back to the field. He approached his coach, Ray Malavasi, and said, "I can play."

Youngblood sat out one drive by the Cowboys, then Coach Malavasi sent him into the game. Youngblood later recalled:

> My first few steps, I thought, "How am I going to beat [Cowboys offensive tackle Rayfield Wright] like this? Not that I can't do it. But how am I gonna do it?" When I tried to explode off the ball, I felt the hindrance, so I just tried to push off the other leg. The amazing thing was, at one point, somehow I got around Rayfield Wright, who in my estimation was one of the three or four premier players I ever played against, a Hall of Fame player. I ran Roger Staubach down for a sack. And we upset the Cowboys to make it to the NFC Championship Game the next week at Tampa.[90]

Sporting a padded cast, Youngblood played in the NFC title game against Tampa Bay the following week. He took painkillers (carefully monitored by his doctors) so that he could play on the broken leg. The Rams shut out the Buccaneers, 9-0.

Next, the Rams faced the Pittsburgh Steelers in Super Bowl XIV at the Rose Bowl in Pasadena. The Rams defense had to stop a legendary Steelers offense that was anchored by quarterback Terry Bradshaw, running back Franco Harris, and wide receivers John Stallworth and Lynn Swann. The pain in Youngblood's broken leg was excruciating, but he didn't care. He was in the Super Bowl, and he intended to play four complete quarters of football.

It was a hard-fought contest, and the Los Angeles Rams led through the first three quarters. Two minutes into the final quarter, however, Bradshaw faked a handoff then dropped back to pass. Jack Youngblood bull-rushed through the Steelers offensive line. Bradshaw stood right in front of him, unprotected, arm cocked to throw a deep pass. For what seemed like an eternity, Bradshaw stood his ground, waiting for his receivers to get open downfield.

Youngblood lunged for Bradshaw—and he was just a split-second too late. Bradshaw launched a pass, which sailed downfield, right into the hands of John Stallworth. The receiver sprinted to the end zone.

Jack Youngblood later concluded that the broken leg had slowed him just enough to keep him from making the play on Bradshaw. Later in the quarter, Franco Harris sealed the game with another Steelers touchdown. Final score: Steelers 31, Rams 19.

Did Youngblood regret playing in the Super Bowl with a broken leg? No way. "The only regret I would have had," he later recalled, "is if I didn't play. I never would have forgiven myself."[91]

Jack Youngblood lives in Orlando today, and I see him every now and then. Whenever I see Jack, I think of what he accomplished, playing in the game of his life on a broken leg. After all these years, his old teammates still speak of him with a sense of awe. They remember him as the Ultimate Teammate, the best teammate anybody ever had. He is a great example of relentless perseverance. If you want to be a great teammate, if you want to live your life without regrets, be a teammate who refuses to quit.

An Indomitable Will

Former football coach Bill Curry describes what it is like to persevere through a grueling final quarter of a hard-fought football game:

> There is a moment in the fourth quarter, when you can't put one foot in front of the other and you've lost fourteen pounds to dehydration and there's blood everywhere and you hadn't missed a play. There is not any money that is going to make you run your face into Dick Butkus. There is not a Super Bowl ring, none of that stuff. It's just some sort of instinct that says I'm indestructible and I'm going to whip this other indestructible guy here. Only then do you see a great team. All the other exterior motives don't work—at some level all you really want to do is quit. So, then, there is some little flame that never flickers and it says *you're not quitting* and it comes from inside. Then you look at the guy next to you and because you love him—you may not particularly like him off the field—but on the field you know what he is and you know what he's going to do. Then, you can't let him down, cannot let him down. That's how great teams happen. ... You're looking for a way to just make yourself put one foot in front of the other.[92]

That's what perseverance feels like. Perseverance is moving forward steadily and relentlessly in spite of obstacles, adversity, pain, discouragement, and even hopelessness. It's the ability to press on even when your body and your emotions are telling you to stop. Perseverance is a state of mind in which you maintain your focus on your goals, even when it seems that your goals are unattainable. Perseverance often achieves victory when victory seems completely out of reach.

I started running marathons when I was 55. In all, I have run 58 marathons, including 13 runnings of the Boston Marathon. People ask me, "Why are you beating up your body like that? You've got to be out of your mind!"

What those people don't understand is that the toughest part of any marathon is not the physical punishment but the mental aspect. A marathon is all about disciplining my mind. For the last 10 miles of a marathon, my body screams at me, "Stop! Quit! Give up!" By running that marathon, I am training my mind to say, "Keep going! Don't quit! Push on!"

So when people ask me why I have run so many marathons, I say, "To practice not quitting. For the last 10 miles, every fiber of my body wants to quit, but my mind forces my body to keep going." When you cross the finish line and they put that medal around your neck, you don't remember the pain. You only feel the exultation.

The lessons of the marathon, the lessons of perseverance, carry through to every aspect of your life. From the marathon, you learn not to quit on your most important relationships. You learn not to quit on God and prayer and your spiritual disciplines. You learn not to quit when your business falls on tough times. You learn not to quit when the doctor says, "You have cancer." You learn to persevere, and to never give up. Marathoning has been my great teacher in the school of endurance and perseverance.

A fight is never truly over until one side surrenders. As long as you are on the side that keeps fighting, you have a chance to win. Once you have decided that quitting is not an option, you're halfway to victory. There is a very good chance that your opponent has not made that decision, even though the opposition seems to have the upper hand. If you decide that you're going to keep fighting, even if you're running on empty, you are not defeated. You can still win this fight.

Every time you press on in the face of discouragement and seemingly hopeless odds, you cement a habit of perseverance into your character. You build courage, self-discipline, pride, and tenacity into your soul. The more you persevere in the face of adversity, the harder it becomes to quit. The harder it is to quit, the greater your odds of success.

When your teammates see you persevering through discouragement, pain, and overwhelming odds, they will be inspired to fight on as well. When you show them that you're totally committed, that you refuse to quit, that you will not surrender, you stiffen their resolve and inspire them to go the distance. Sometimes the fate of an entire team hinges on the unyielding will of one member of that team. You can be that person on your team. You can be the one who refuses to quit. You can be the one who inspires your team to win.

As the late, great Reggie White put it: "Don't give up! Don't let anything or anyone stop you. Do what is right and do the work God has given you to do. Very few touchdowns are made with a single 99-yard pass. Most touchdowns come at the end of a ten- or fifteen-down drive made up of five-yard plays, three-yard plays, and even lost yards."[93]

You may not be the most talented or skilled player on your team. You may not be the strongest or the fastest. But you can be the one who refuses to quit. You can be the one who inspires your teammates to fight on. It doesn't take talent or skill to persevere. It only takes an indomitable will.

"You can't live scared."

The amazing switch-hitting centerfielder Mickey Mantle was born in Oklahoma, the son of Elvin "Mutt" Mantle, a hard-working man who toiled in the lead mines. Mutt taught Mickey to love baseball from an early age and he hoped that baseball would be Mickey's ticket out of the mines.

Mickey Mantle began his playing career with the semi-pro Baxter Springs Whiz Kids of Kansas. In 1948, a Yankees scout attended a Whiz Kids game in which Mantle hit three homers. The scout signed Mantle to a contract that would make a pro baseball player of him as soon as he graduated from high school. Mantle played for a farm club, the Independence Yankees, for two years, then he was called up to the Yankees instructional camp before the 1951 season. Manager Casey Stengel was impressed with the young player and promoted Mantle to the majors.

Though he was a powerful hitter, Mickey Mantle had a hard time handling the mental aspect of the game. The pressure to perform caused him to lose his mental focus. Mantle had a brief and disappointing stint in the majors before Stengel sent him to the Yankees' top farm team, the Kansas City Blues. There he went into a disastrous slump. It appeared that all the promise he had shown in the lower minors would never be fulfilled.

The frustrated 19-year-old Mickey Mantle called his father in Commerce, Oklahoma. Mickey told Mutt that his career was over, and he had decided to quit baseball for good.

Mutt had been following Mickey's career in the newspapers, and he knew his son was struggling. But Mutt was convinced that Mickey was just going through a temporary slump. The young man could pull out of the slump if he refused to give up. So Mutt jumped in his car and drove five hours from Oklahoma to Kansas City to talk some sense into his son.

Mickey Mantle later recalled, "I wanted him to pat me on the back and cheer me up and tell me how badly the Yankees had treated me and all that sort of stuff. I guess I was like a little boy, and I wanted him to comfort me."

But Mutt Mantle had other plans. When Mickey again told him he planned to quit baseball, Mutt replied, "Well, Mick, if that's all the guts you have, I think you better quit. You might as well come home right now. … Baseball is no different than any other job. Things get tough once in a while, and you must learn how to take it—the sooner, the better. It takes guts, not moaning, to make it. And if that's all the guts you have, I agree with you. You don't belong in baseball. Come on back to Commerce and grub out a living in the mines for the rest of your life. I thought I raised a man, not a coward."

Those words tore Mickey Mantle's heart out—yet Mickey later told an interviewer that his father's lecture was "the greatest thing my father ever did for me." Mutt's words put everything in perspective. Mickey later recalled:

> All the encouragement he had given me when I was small, all the sacrifices he made so I could play ball when other boys were working in the mines, all the painstaking instruction he had provided—all of these would have been thrown away if he had not been there that night to put the iron into my spine when it was needed most. I never felt as ashamed as I did then, to hear my father sound disappointed in me. … He didn't give me any inspiring speeches. … All he did was show me that I was acting scared, and that you can't live scared.[94]

Immediately after Mutt visited Mickey and gave him that talk, Mickey broke out of his slump. He went on to hit .361 with Kansas City, including 11 homers and 50 RBIs. The Yankees called him up to the majors during the season, and he went on to hit .267 with 13 home runs and 65 RBIs in 96 games.

Mickey Mantle ultimately became one of the legendary players of the game, with a lifetime batting average of .298, 536 career home runs, 2,415 career hits, and 1,509 career RBIs. He played for the New York Yankees from 1951 through 1968, was a 20-time All-Star, helped the Yankees win seven World Series championships, and was American League MVP in 1956, 1957, and 1962.

But first, he had to learn a lesson from his father: it takes guts and perseverance to make it in any worthwhile endeavor. Never surrender. Never give up. Be the kind of teammate who never quits and you'll be the best teammate anybody ever had.

12 BE PASSIONATE!

"It was about my passion for the game. I just loved it. I absolutely loved to compete and to step out onto that football field with my teammates."

—Former Quarterback Warren Moon

Former Magic head coach Stan Van Gundy told me the following:

> Jameer Nelson is a rare guy who is as excited for the team's success as he is for his own. He has a passion for the game and for this team. He wants to see others succeed, so he's always thinking about his teammates. Because of that passion and excitement, Jameer has a very good perspective on people and will often go speak with a guy if he senses the player is struggling with a problem. He is always there for the other guys, through good times and bad. That's how he's managed to develop such a great relationship of trust and rapport with his teammates.

When you watch Jameer play basketball, you see enthusiasm, excitement, and passion on the court. He can elevate the intensity of the entire team with his passion for the game, his passion for winning. That's why Jameer Nelson is a role model for teammates everywhere, in every sport and at every level.

To be the best teammate anybody ever had, be passionate and enthusiastic at all times. Let your intense emotion inspire and motivate everyone around you. Be known as the person who always had fun on the court or the field. Whatever your sport, remember that it's still a game, so play for the thrill of it, the fun of it, the passion of competing and winning. If it stops being fun, if you no longer have the passion, why play the game?

Passion Is Extreme Emotion

Andy Russell is a former linebacker who played his entire 12-year career with the Pittsburgh Steelers. A mainstay of the dreaded "Steel Curtain" defense, Russell recalls an experience that impacted him in his rookie year. During a hard-fought game, he was in the huddle alongside defensive lineman Ernie Stautner. To his horror, Andy Russell saw that Stautner's thumb was broken at the base. A bloody stump of bone protruded through the torn flesh. As Russell watched, Stautner wrenched his thumb and tucked it into his fist to keep the skin from tearing any more. Stautner didn't say a word about his broken thumb and didn't show it to anyone. With a look of intensity in his eyes, he asked, "What's the defense?"

Later, on the sidelines, Andy Russell kept an eye on Ernie Stautner and his busted thumb. Russell thought the defensive lineman would leave the game to have his thumb treated. But that's not what happened.

"Give me some tape," Stautner told one of the Steelers trainers. Andy Russell felt sick to his stomach as he watched Stautner wind several rolls of tape around his fist until it was like a club. After his hand was taped up, Stautner went back onto the field and played every down.

"After the game," Russell recalled, "I watched as the doctor cut off the tape. Blood trickled from the wound. ... I thought, *What kind of man could ignore a compound fracture? Doesn't he feel pain like the rest of us? Maybe,* I worried, *I don't belong in the NFL.*"

What compelled Ernie Stautner to play through the pain of a partially severed thumb? According to Andy Russell, it was Stautner's passion for the game. "That is passion for what you do," Russell concluded. "That guy was making no money. He just loved to play."[95]

Great teammates know that pain is temporary, but the passion for winning lasts a lifetime. In his book *Beyond Basketball: Coach K's Keywords for Success*, Duke basketball coach Mike Krzyzewski wrote:

> When I have speaking engagements, I often tell my audience how lucky I am to have never had a job. … Because I have always done what I love to do, I have never considered my work a job. I have merely been pursuing my passion and loving every minute of it.
>
> I define passion as extreme emotion. When you are passionate, you always have your destination in sight and you are not distracted by obstacles. Because you love what you are pursuing, things like rejection and setbacks will not hinder you in your pursuit. You believe that nothing can stop you![96]

A few years ago, I attended an NBA lottery dinner event and sat at a table with ESPN college broadcaster Jay Bilas. Jay had been in Coach Krzyzewski's first recruiting class at Duke in the early 1980s. I said, "Jay, tell me your most vivid memory of Coach Krzyzewski." Bilas said:

> During my freshman year, we had a practice the day before a big game. We gathered in the locker room, and Coach K stood in front of us in his blue Duke coaching shorts and golf shirt. He started talking to us about the big game, and he was all pumped up and excited. As I listened to him talk, I noticed he had goose-bumps all over his legs, his arms, his neck. The man was just a mass of goose-bumps! Twenty-five years later, I can still see that image in my mind—an image of Coach K, a man who was so passionate about basketball that he got goose-bumps just talking about it.

That kind of passion can't be faked or manufactured. You've got to feel it. You've got to live it. You've got to believe it. That's an emotion so strong you can't contain it.

Passion Makes a Great Competitor

When Jon Gruden coached the Tampa Bay Buccaneers, he told a writer for *Sports Illustrated*: "I love the strategy. I love being around the guys. I like the competition. I love flying home after a big win, the locker room celebrations. I like to see how we all act in the face of adversity. Are we going to throw our helmets, or are we going to find a way out of this? Is it going to be second-and-nine or first-and-ten? Are we going to make this field goal? What's the weather going to be like tomorrow for the game? I wonder if it's going to be a loud crowd. … I just like the thrill of it all."[97]

Do you know that feeling? Do you nod your head in agreement as you read about Jon Gruden's passion for the game? Do you feel a tingling inside just thinking about playing your game, whether your game is football, baseball, basketball, or Olympic ice curling? Then you have the passion, the extreme emotion, of a great competitor, a great teammate.

In the 1990s, I attended a banquet in Orlando with sports agent Mark McCormack and his wife Betsy. Also at our table was Winnie Palmer, wife of golfer Arnold Palmer. Winnie was a charming and engaging woman, and I enjoyed talking with her that evening (and I was sorry to hear, a few years after this event, that she passed away). I asked her to explain what made Arnold Palmer such a unique individual. She said:

> Arnie wakes up every morning, ready to charge into the day, full-speed ahead. He's absolutely passionate about tackling his projects and getting things done. He always has a long list of things to do, and he lives every day to the fullest, like it's his last day on earth. Another special quality of Arnie's is his love for people. He genuinely cares for his fans, just as much as they care for him. He has a passion for making his fans happy and giving each one his personal attention. He will never leave after a match until he has signed every autograph.

Do you have that kind of passion for living, passion for competing, passion for making the fans happy? If you do, then you have the passion of a great teammate.

Passion makes a great competitor. Passion compels us to prepare ourselves, to focus on our goals, to fight hard on the field of competition, to persevere until we have nothing left to give. My friend Ernie Accorsi, former general manager of the New York Giants, put it this way: "When a big game is decided or a championship is on the line, the game is going to go to the players who love the game more than the other players. It will go to those who play with emotion."

Marques Johnson was a five-time All-Star during his NBA career, which lasted from 1977 to 1989. He played most of his career with the Milwaukee Bucks. In a 1980 interview for *Sports Illustrated*, Johnson described his own passion for the game:

> It's the sport that I love, not the business. The business end messes everything up. I almost wish there was no money in it, then we could all go out and enjoy playing like we did when we were kids. I'd still play if there was no money, because it's the best game there is, and you can play all the time if you want. Anybody who's ever been into it, pro or playground, knows what I'm talking about. When I'm playing ball, it's like I'm not even part of the earth—like I belong to a different universe.[98]

That kind of extreme emotion spills over into every aspect of the game, even practices. NFL quarterback Peyton Manning expressed his passion for the game this way: "For me, it's not just about the game, I mean I love practice. A lot of guys don't. I like going to practice. I love ... taking the game plan and putting it to work on Sunday."[99]

Passion Equals Enthusiasm

Retired Florida State football coach Bobby Bowden equates passion with enthusiasm. He observed: "Enthusiasm makes a player jump higher, hit harder, and run faster."[100]

Bowden adds, "I like for my players to show enthusiasm on the field." Why? Because Bowden understands that enthusiasm—extreme emotion—is contagious. It quickly spreads to other players and elevates the intensity of the entire team.

Coach Bowden cites the example of Corey Simon, who was a passionate, emotional, motivational player on Florida State's 1999 national championship football team. "He could really arouse enthusiasm among his teammates," Bowden recalled. "I think part of his motivational success lay in the fact that he could physically handle just about anyone on the team, and they knew it. So when he said, 'Let's work hard,' they worked hard. It helps to have one or two folks in the trenches were both excitable and respected by their peers."[101]

Great teammates have that kind of impact on one another. They inspire passion and enthusiasm. They motivate and fire each other up with a passion for greatness. They get up each morning, inspired and eager to take on the challenges of the day. Their eyes are alight with optimism. Their voices reverberate with energy and emotion. Their gestures and body language make the air around them tingle with electricity. They radiate excitement and intensity. They communicate with passionate words and ideas.

When you have a passionate team that is excited about competing and intensely committed to winning, there are no limits to what you can achieve. A passionate player is going to play his heart out. Passionate people are mentally tough, and refuse to quit. They love the game so much that even the physical pain and exhaustion of competition bring them a kind of joy.

If you add passion to all the other ingredients that make up the Ultimate Teammate, you have a player who is almost impossible to defeat. You can't stop him. You can't wear him down. You can't make him surrender. His passion will keep him going far beyond the normal limits of human endurance.

Great teammates don't play for money or championships or glory or praise from the coach or the roar of the crowd. Great teammates are simply passionate about the game. They play out of extreme, uninhibited, uncontainable emotion.

Be a player of passion and enthusiasm, and you'll be the best teammate anybody ever had.

13

STAY
HUMBLE

"Talent is God-given. Be humble. Fame is man-given. Be grateful. Conceit is self-given. Be careful."

—Coach John Wooden

XiXinXing/iStock/Thinkstock

Before Jameer Nelson arrived at Saint Joseph's, head basketball coach Phil Martelli's Hawks struggled through three consecutive losing seasons. In the final game of the 1999–2000 regular season, Saint Joseph's was demolished by Xavier, 94-66. After the game, Coach Martelli's phone rang. The caller was Jameer Nelson, then a senior at Chester High School who had agreed to play for Saint Joseph's the following season.

Jameer asked, "Coach, are you all right?" The high school player was worried that his future coach was feeling discouraged by the drubbing at the hands of Xavier.

Coach Martelli said that he was holding up despite the disappointment.

"The losing will stop when I get there," Jameer said.

Now, if anyone else but Jameer Nelson had said those words, they would have sounded arrogant. But Jameer wasn't being arrogant. He's truly one of the most humble players I've ever met at any level of the game.

Jameer Nelson is that rare combination of traits—a young player with great skills and great confidence combined with great humility. He is aware of his talent and ability, but he has never let it go to his head. The true benchmark of his humility is the fact that, in spite of all of his achievements, awards, and media attention, Jameer has remained grounded. He always puts his teammates ahead of himself and his own ego.

One of Jameer's teammates at Saint Joe's, Rob Sullivan, told an interviewer, "His humility really stood out to me. With all the notoriety that he was given—and well-deserved because of his basketball game—the media didn't know what type of person he was in the locker room. He was humble, modest, and he just brought a great joy into the locker room."[102]

Coach Martelli shared with me an incident that speaks volumes about the humble attitude of Jameer Nelson:

> Before road games, the team would normally go out to eat at a restaurant. Jameer was uncomfortable with all the attention he got, so he said, 'Coach, let's just eat in the hotel restaurant.' Sometimes the fans can say things that are a bit thoughtless, yet Jameer always dealt with their comments cheerfully and with good-natured humility. Once, when a lady said to him, "You're kind of short to be a basketball player," Jameer replied, "Yeah, I'm the water boy—but I'm the best water boy in the country!"

And Rob Sullivan told me: "Jameer's humble approach is out of this world. He has the ability to connect with teammates, fans, sportswriters, and everyone else. That's his greatest attribute."

Humility builds teams. An outsized ego can destroy a talented team, but humility and unselfishness can enable a less talented team to overachieve. So stay grounded. Don't get a big head. Don't alienate your teammates. The Ultimate Teammate is a humble teammate.

Humble People Know Who They Are

The Magic played the Knicks at home a couple of days before Christmas 2013. Our phenomenal rookie shooting guard, Victor Oladipo, who was the number-two pick in the NBA draft, played in the first half of the game but didn't play at all in the second half, simply because that's that way the game was flowing. But even when Oladipo was off the court, he was far from idle.

What was he doing? Oladipo decided to be the self-appointed Orlando Magic assistant trainer. He distributed water to his teammates during the time-outs. Why did he do that? As he put it, "I just wanted to keep our guys hydrated."

Seeing the humble way Victor Oladipo served his teammates, I thought, *Wow! The number-two NBA draft pick is willing to be the water boy. He's willing to serve his teammates any way he can, whether it's shooting from the field or handing out cups of cold water. With both Jameer Nelson and Victor Oladipo on our team, we've got at least two guys who are the best teammates anybody ever had!*

I once paid a visit to the office of Jerry Colangelo when he was the owner and president of the Phoenix Suns. Three special artifacts in his office riveted my attention. The first was a photo of the humble Chicago Heights home where Jerry grew up, partially constructed with wood siding from a railroad box car. The second was an ancient Roman amphora, more than 2,000 years old, used for storing olive oil—a reminder of Jerry's Italian heritage. The third was an old accordion that Jerry's grandfather had taught him to play—a reminder of his simple, happy childhood.

I asked Jerry what those three artifacts meant to him, and he said, "These three objects help me maintain my perspective on life. They remind me of where I came from and how far I've come—and they teach me to stay humble. Everything I have is a gift, and it could all vanish." He snapped his fingers. "Just like that."

Again and again over the years, I've seen players begin their careers as humble, decent, likable people, only to lose their humility along the way. Many players begin to believe their press clippings and the adulation of their fans. They start thinking they are a cut above mere mortals. They become narcissistic and drunk with power and popularity. It goes to their heads. It inflates their egos.

A lot of great team chemistry has been wrecked by the arrogance of one or two players. Looking back, I recall some of the cocky, full-of-themselves teammates I've played with, and I just didn't want to be around them anymore. Nobody does.

Humility is the lubricant of great teams. A humble attitude reduces friction, generates unselfishness, and enables the various parts of a team to function harmoniously together. Arrogance is like sand tossed into the team mechanism, causing abrasion, dysfunction, and breakdown. You can't build a functioning team out of a bunch of self-centered egos. Teamwork is the result of a pervasive attitude of humility.

Humble players view all of their teammates as equals, never as inferior. Humble players are willing to be held accountable by their teammates. Humble players die to self and crucify their own egos for the sake of the team. Humble players are teachable and coachable, because they want to learn and grow. They ask for help and seek out advice. They pay their dues and eagerly accept coaching and instruction.

Some people mistake humility for humiliation—a sense of unworthiness or even worthlessness. But that's not true humility. Genuinely humble people have confidence and a healthy sense of self-esteem. They are secure in their abilities and accomplishments—so secure, in fact, that they never feel the need to impress others or prove themselves better than others.

When Jameer Nelson told Coach Martelli, "The losing will stop when I get there," he wasn't being cocky or arrogant. Jameer knew the contribution he was capable of making at St. Joe's—but he wasn't going to be uncoachable, and he wasn't going to be arrogant and demanding. He was simply going to play his role and be the best teammate anybody ever had. Simply by playing his role, he'd make sure the losing would stop.

It's okay to be confident—just don't lord it over others. Don't be bossy. Don't flaunt your ability and accomplishments. Play confidently but unselfishly. Be sure to pass the ball to the teammate who's in the best position to make the shot. And if you're the player with the open shot, go ahead and take it.

Someone once said that genuine humility doesn't make you think less of yourself; it simply makes you think of yourself less. Most of the truly humble people I've known had dynamic, unforgettable personalities. Their humility attracted others to them. Fact is, arrogance and vanity are off-putting to people. Confidence combined with genuine humility is one of the most attractive combinations of traits any human being could ever possess.

Humility is a form of strength, not weakness. It's the ability to put others ahead of oneself. A humble person's ego cannot be inflated by praise or deflated by criticism. Accolades and insults alike roll off of humble people like water off a duck's back, because their self-esteem doesn't depend on what other people say to them or about them. Mother Theresa once put it this way: "If you are humble, nothing can touch you, neither praise nor disgrace, because you know who you are."

Role Models of Humility

Longtime college basketball broadcaster (and my longtime friend) Billy Packer once told me, "John Wooden is the most humble famous person I have ever met." I couldn't agree more.

Years ago, when I was preparing to write a book called *How to Be Like Coach Wooden*, I wrote to him and asked for his blessing on the project. Days later, he called me and said, "Mr. Williams, this is John Wooden, the former basketball coach at UCLA. I received your letter, and even though I'm not worthy of a project like this, if you would like to write this book, you go right ahead."

The first words he spoke to me were words of total humility. That phone call was the beginning of a decade-long relationship with Coach Wooden. Over the years since then, I have written three books on his life and his philosophy. I always looked forward to my visits with Coach Wooden, and I came away from every encounter with a renewed sense of his humble and self-effacing nature.

A sports reporter once interviewed Coach Wooden, referring to him as "a legend" and calling him by a nickname that sportswriters had hung on him: "The Wizard of Westwood." Coach Wooden immediately corrected the reporter. "I'm no legend," he said, "and I am embarrassed [to be called] that. I don't like the 'Wizard' [title] at all. I don't like false modesty. I'm proud of the fact that I was fortunate to have a lot of wonderful players who brought about national championships and that I'm a part of that. ... But I'm also realistic, and I know that without those players it wouldn't have happened."[103] Coach John Wooden always turned the spotlight away from himself and onto his players.

His humility was not a pose, not a put-on. He continued to act humbly even when no one else was watching. College basketball coach Bob Burke told me a story about Coach Wooden's humble nature. "Back in the 1960s," Bob said, "I was working on the staff at the Campbell University summer camp. On the first day, I went out early to get oriented, and there was John Wooden, championship coach, sweeping the floor all by himself."

In 2003, Coach John Wooden went to the White House where he received the Presidential Medal of Freedom from President George W. Bush. Later, Coach Wooden said, "I couldn't believe I was there. I am just a simple farm boy." Yet that "simple farm boy" happens to be the man the *Sporting News* selected as the greatest coach in any sport, in any level, of all time. He didn't seem to be aware of his own greatness—and he certainly wasn't changed by it. He thought of himself in simple, humble terms—and that is what made him so great.

Ken Whitten is the senior pastor of Idlewild Baptist Church in Tampa, Florida, and for a number of years he was pastor to Coach Tony Dungy, who retired in 2008 as head coach of the Indianapolis Colts. Pastor Whitten told me a story that took place shortly after Coach Dungy's son James committed suicide at age 18. A few days before Christmas 2005, a man came to Tony and said, "I'm desperate to keep my son from taking his life. His fiancée recently committed suicide, and he's depressed and sees no hope for his future. Could you call him and give him a word of hope?"

Coach Dungy called the young man and said, "My name is Tony. Your father asked me to talk to you." They talked for a long time, and Coach Dungy described his own intense grief after the death of his son.

"You know," Tony concluded, "I don't know why God let my son die. But maybe He allowed this sorrow in my life so that I could talk to you now and tell you, 'Don't do that to your daddy.'" Coach Dungy asked the young man to promise to call him in the morning.

"Okay," the young man said, "I give you my word. I'll call you in the morning."

Tony continued to talk with him by phone every day for a week. Finally, the young man told Tony he was doing better, and he promised he wouldn't commit suicide. Then the young man asked Coach Dungy, "Tony, what do you do for a living?" The young man didn't even know he'd been speaking to one of the most famous coaches in the NFL!

Dungy replied, "I'm a football coach."

"Really? Do you coach high school or college football?"

"I coach the Indianapolis Colts."

Only then did the young man realize who he was talking to. Humility doesn't say, "Look at me. Look at how important I am." Humility says, "Tell me about yourself. Tell me where you're hurting. How can I help you? How can I serve you?"

That should be our attitude toward our teammates, and toward everyone else we encounter. Instead of making ourselves out to be important, let's make others feel important and empowered and cared for. Let's humbly reach out to others and serve them to the best of our ability. That is how to become the best teammate anybody ever had.

Lessons in Humility

Born in a railway boxcar and raised poor in Illinois, Mannie Jackson grew up to become the owner and chairman of the Harlem Globetrotters—and the first African-American to own a major international sports organization. He purchased the nearly bankrupt Globetrotters in 1993, and engineered one of the most dramatic turnarounds in the American sports business history. Under his leadership, the Globetrotters organization increased revenue five-fold and rebuilt its fan base to previously unheard-of levels. The team now entertains more than two million attendees every year.

In spite of these achievements, Mannie is humble and eager to share credit with others. "I would not be where I am today," Mannie told me, "without the support and encouragement of my parents and my high school basketball coach, Joe Lucco. Coach Lucco pushed me to be my best, both on and off the court. The discipline and attitude I learned from Coach Lucco have made me a better business executive and have directly contributed to the revival of the Harlem Globetrotters."

Mannie told me how Coach Lucco taught him the importance of humility:

Coach Lucco was a strict mentor regarding personal appearance. Coach wanted us to work together and be a team, not a loose collection of individual stars. That was tough for me at the time, because I was the captain and the leading scorer of the basketball team, and I liked to dress flamboyantly. One of my signature items of clothing was a fedora. When I first got it, I wore it everywhere.

One day, I boarded the team bus for the trip to another school for a game. I was dressed in my resplendent style, including my fedora. Coach took one look at me and sent me home to change. I did what I was told, but when I returned to the school parking lot, the bus was gone.

I took a cab to the other school. At the time, I was working part-time jobs and didn't have extra money for cab fare. Arriving at the school, I went to Coach Lucco and said, "It cost me nine bucks in cab fare to get here." He said, "I'll make you a deal: you score 30 points and we win this game, and I'll pay your cab fare. Deal?"

That night, I scored over 30 points by the third quarter, and we won the game. Coach gave me my nine bucks. This taught me an important lesson: no matter how important you think you are, when you're part of a team, you respect the rules and the other people on the team. Nobody is bigger than the organization. Nobody's a big shot. I needed that lesson in humility—and I never wore my fedora on the team bus again.

Longtime Major League shortstop and manager Alvin Dark shared with me a lesson in humility he learned early in his career:

I was with the Boston Braves, and Johnny Cooney was the manager of the team. Late in the game, he took me out and sent in a pinch hitter. I went berserk! I took my bat and went to into a little room behind the dugout. There was a wooden wheelbarrow in that room, and I started smashing that wheelbarrow to bits with my bat. It sounded like a rifle shot every time I hit that thing. I was totally out of control.

After the game, I was sitting on a stool in front of my locker. My teammate, Eddie Stanky, sidled over to me, and said very quietly, "So you're Babe Ruth, huh? Not allowed to pinch-hit for you, huh?" I could have pinched Stanky's head off—but he was right. I learned a great lesson in humility that day.

Bart Lundy is head coach for men's basketball at Queens University of Charlotte. He once told me of a young player he coached at High Point University in High Point, North Carolina. The player's name was Danny Gathings. Lundy said:

During the time Danny was at High Point, he underwent more growth as a person than any other player I ever coached. When he arrived, everyone expected him to fail. By the time he finished his education at High Point, he was a role model for other kids growing up in difficult, underprivileged conditions.

I remember standing with Danny at a convocation service on the campus of Liberty University, one of our conference rivals. There, he received the Big South Tournament plaque for Most Valuable Player—and then he turned right around and handed it to Liberty University guard Larry Blair. Why did he give the award away to a player from a rival team? Because he believed Larry Blair had truly earned it.

A few days before that ceremony, Danny came to me and said, "Coach, I didn't earn that award. Larry Blair deserves it." He'd worked out the numbers for the three Big South tournament games. Danny had averaged 11.7 points per game and shot 16 for 29 (55.2 percent) from the field. Great stats—but Danny figured out that Blair had averaged 21 points per game and shot 24 for 43 (55.8 percent) from the field. Blair also shot a tournament-record seven three-pointers in the championship game—a game in which Liberty beat High Point 89 to 44. Danny looked at the numbers and decided to give the award to Blair. He said, "Coach, I need to do this. Larry deserves the award, and I'm happy to honor his efforts. Hopefully, I'll deserve it next year."

Well, the moment Danny handed over that award, he received a standing ovation from the Liberty students—probably the first, last, and only time I'll ever see the students of a rival school applaud my best player. I was stunned and choked up. As a result of this humble gesture on Danny's part, the NCAA gave him the sportsmanship award that year.

To be the best teammate anybody has ever had, and to truly be the Ultimate Teammate, stay humble. Put others first. Think *team*, not self. If you want to have a powerful, positive impact on your teammates and on everyone around you, be a role model of humility.

14 RESPECT
YOUR TEAMMATES

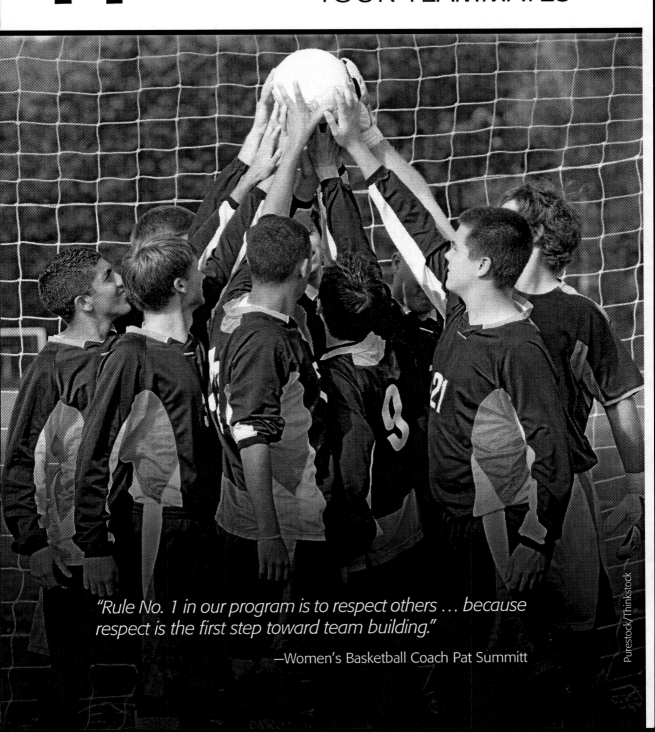

"Rule No. 1 in our program is to respect others ... because respect is the first step toward team building."

—Women's Basketball Coach Pat Summitt

Purestock/Thinkstock

In November 2013, scandal erupted over a pattern of brutal hazing and threats by Miami Dolphins guard Richie Incognito against a teammate, offensive tackle Jonathan Martin. The Dolphins suspended Incognito for "conduct detrimental to the team."

A few days after the scandal broke, Jameer Nelson, then in his 10th season with the Orlando Magic, went in front of reporters to talk about the problem of bullying and hazing in professional sports. He said:

> A team is put together so that guys can work together, and so they can have a healthy environment. … Whether it's emotionally, spiritually, racially, whatever, we're here together. We work together. And we're trying to build a team. When guys on your team are down, you try to pick them up. You don't put your foot on their throat and try to hold them down. You've got to keep them up as much as possible and have each other's back. …
>
> Everybody will tell you, I'm a joker. But I know when to joke and when not to joke, what to say and what not to say. As a member of the team, my job is to help my teammates out, not shoot them down. We're in this together. We win together, we lose together. We're a really close group, like a family. We spend more time with each other than with our own families, so we should look on each other as brothers.[104]

I was proud to see Jameer come out and make such a strong statement to the press. Great teams run on mutual respect, not fear or abuse or hazing. Jameer described the kind of team all of us want the Orlando Magic to be, the kind of values we want the team to project to the world. And Jameer himself has always embodied those values, which is why he is the Ultimate Teammate.

Saint Joseph's assistant coach Rob Sullivan was a sophomore at St. Joe's in 2003–2004 when Jameer was a senior. He told me: "Underlying everything Jameer did was a foundation of respect for his teammates, from player one to player sixteen. By working hard and treating his teammates with respect, he commanded respect from all of us. We thought, 'If the best college player in the country is working this hard, how can I slack off?' That's how Jameer was able to get so much effort out of his teammates."

It all comes down to mutual respect. A team isn't a team without tightly bonded mutual relationships. Team relationships are built on mutual respect.

Respect the Game

A team cannot operate successfully without respect. On every team, there will be personality clashes, contrasts in style and approach, and differences of opinion. Despite these differences, a team must be unified so it can function as a unit. A team's diversity—its many personality types and skill sets and areas of specialization—can be its greatest strength, but only if each player respects all of his fellow teammates. Without respect, a team's diversity will become a self-destructive force.

The goal of teamwork is not to force everybody to think alike. Teamwork entails a respect for diversity while enabling people to transcend their differences so they can unite behind a common goal. It's okay if players argue hard for their ideas and points of view, as long as they can respect each other amid their differences.

Coach John Wooden taught his players to respect each other and to be respectful wherever they went. He once told a reporter:

> I like to make spot checks on lockers and see they're not getting slovenly. Wherever we are, we will leave our dressing rooms every bit as neat as when we came in. There will be no gum wrappers on the floor. No tape scattered around. No orange peels. They'll all be placed in a container. And I don't expect our manager to be the pick-up man. Our players understand this.
>
> I help. If I start picking things up, the players soon join in. We'll have equipment managers around the country tell us no one leaves the dressing room like we do. Well, I think that's part of better basketball. Now I'd have a hard time proving that, but I think it is. I think it gives us a little more unity, a sense of doing things together, of showing consideration for the other fellow. The waitress at the hotel here said this was the finest, best-behaved group of athletes she's had. Our players complimented her on the way she'd been serving them. She could hardly believe it.[105]

Ryne Sandberg played second base for the Chicago Cubs and retired with a .989 career fielding percentage—a Major League Baseball record for that position. When he was inducted into the Baseball Hall of Fame in 2005, he talked about respect for the game and for one's teammates:

> People say this honor validates my career, but I didn't work hard for validation. I didn't play the game right because I saw a reward at the end of the tunnel. I played it right because that's what you're supposed to do—play it right and with respect. …
>
> You see players self-promoting. They hit a home run, their team is still down four or five runs, and here they are tipping their hat to the camera because they hit a home run. It drives me nuts. … I'd like to see more of a team concept. We, not I. …
>
> I was in awe every time I walked onto the field. That's respect. I was taught you never, ever disrespect your opponents or your teammates, your organization, your manager, and never your uniform. Make a great

play, act like you've done it before. Get a big hit, look for the third-base coach and be ready to run the bases. Hit a home run, put your head down, drop the bat, run around the bases because the name on the front is a lot more important than the name on the back.[106]

What is respect? It is an attitude of honor and consideration toward another person. To show respect doesn't mean you necessarily *like* that person. You can respect your teammates even if you dislike them and disagree with them. You can even respect your opponents. You can respect the traffic policeman who stopped you, even if you are sure you don't deserve a ticket. You can respect the president, even if you didn't vote for him. And you can respect your coach, even if you think he's unfair and doesn't know his Xs from his Os. Respect is the unconditional acceptance and consideration we show to one another so that a diverse collection of individuals can be forged together into a functioning team.

In his speech, Ryne Sandberg also talked about respect for the game. He said: "The reason I am here, they tell me, is that I played the game a certain way, that I played the game the way it was supposed to be played. I don't know about that, but I do know this: I had too much respect for the game to play it any other way."[107]

Respect for the game is a key concept in the teamwork realm. What does it mean to respect the game? It means that we honor the rules, traditions, and code of the game we play. We consider it a privilege to play that game at any level, and we refuse to do anything that would disgrace that game.

When Tom Kelly stepped down as manager of the Minnesota Twins in 2002, he was replaced by my friend Ron Gardenhire. I was president of the Twins AA affiliate in Orlando when Ron managed the club in 1990 (Ron even lived in our guesthouse). When *USA Today* asked about the lessons Ron had learned from Tom Kelly, Ron Gardenhire replied:

> Make sure that you always respect the game—and that your players respect the game. You can't believe how many speeches I've heard from Tom Kelly talking about respecting the game. When I first heard it, I said: "Let's think about that. What does he mean, respect the game?" Well, now I know what it means. It's about going out and never leaving anything behind. You go out, don't take the game for granted or it will kick you right in the butt—guaranteed, it will. ... You give everything you have that day.[108]

One baseball player who respected the game and respected everyone he encountered was shortstop Derek Jeter, who spent his entire career with the New York Yankees. Known for his polite manner (he always addressed coaches and managers as "Mr." or "sir"), he learned a respectful attitude from his father, psychologist Charles Jeter. Once, when young Derek was in Little League, his team lost and he sullenly refused to shake hands with his opponents. So Charles told Derek, "Son, it's time to grab a tennis racket, since you don't know how to play a team sport." It was a lesson in respect that stuck with Derek Jeter and still guides his behavior to this day.[109]

Respect Leads to Trust; Trust Leads to Loyalty

Back in 1996, the Orlando Magic was in the Eastern Conference Finals in the playoffs. The Magic would eventually fall to the Chicago Bulls in four straight games. Shortly before game three in the Orlando Arena, I was chatting outside the Bulls locker room with John Heffernon, who served as the Bulls' team physician throughout the Jordan era. I said, "Doc, 20 years from now, what are you going to remember most about Michael Jordan?"

He said, "Aside from the fact that he is the most competitive human being ever to walk the face of the earth and has absolutely no fear of failure, what I'll remember most is that he respected everybody the same. It didn't matter if you were the president or the ball boy, the Pope or the equipment manager, he treated everybody with equal respect."

Duke University basketball coach Mike Krzyzewski recalls serving as assistant to head coach Chuck Daly on the 1992 Olympic Dream Team. It was the first time NBA players were allowed to play in the Olympics. Michael Jordan was on that team, and he was at the peak of his stardom. Krzyzewski was impressed that Jordan always addressed him with the utmost respect. Jordan would ask, "Coach, would you stay and work with me on my shooting? Thank you, Coach. I appreciate it." This went on throughout the entire Olympic period.

Mike Krzyzewski will tell you that this demonstration of respect from the greatest player in the world touched him deeply. Michael Jordan gave Mike Krzyzewski a degree of respect he never dreamed he'd receive from a player of Jordan's caliber. When players show respect to coaches and to their teammates, they create a bond of significance that will never be forgotten. One of the most important gifts you can give to any other human being is the gift of respect, because respect is foundational to all human relationships.

Respect leads to trust. When you respect your teammates' abilities and their character, you *know* you have teammates you can trust. Trust leads to loyalty. When you and your teammates learn to trust each other through times of adversity and victory, you create strong, mutual ties of loyalty. You are able to say, "I've been through good times and bad with these teammates, and we've never let each other down. We are a team." That kind of loyalty leads to love. When you and your teammates prove your mutual loyalty to one another, what else can you feel for one another but love? And that kind of unconditional love produces team relationships—true friendships—that last a lifetime.

So the formula for building the ultimate team is as follows: respect leads to trust; trust leads to loyalty; loyalty leads to love; love leads to friendship.

A true story from the world of mountain-climbing illustrates the key role that respect plays in the team-building process:

Jürgen Schrempp, former CEO of car conglomerate DaimlerChrysler, once climbed the peak known as König Ortler, a 12,812-foot mountain in the Italian Alps. His teammate was mountaineer Reinhold Messner. Jürgen Schrempp had a deep, abiding trust in Messner because of Messner's depth of experience, which included conquering Everest without an oxygen tank. In the course of their climb together, they came to a place where Schrempp would have to descend a rock wall without any handhold or foothold—and it was a long way down to the next ledge.

Schrempp looked up at Messner, who was on a ledge high above him. "Reinhold," he said, "I'm stuck! What if I fall?"

"You're tied on to me," said Messner. "I'd catch you and lower you safely down."

Schrempp nodded—then without a word of warning, he jumped. Messner hadn't expected Schrempp to act so immediately and with such complete trust—but the rope held, and Messner lowered Schrempp safely to the next ledge.[110]

Jürgen Schrempp's respect for Reinhold Messner led to absolute trust—a trust so great he was willing to take a leap of faith off a mountain ledge, trusting that Messner would not let him fall to his death. Respect leads to trust. When you respect your teammates' abilities and character, you *know* you have teammates you can trust.

Next, trust leads to loyalty. When you and your teammates earn one another's trust by going through crises and adversity together, you forge unbreakable bonds of loyalty. You know you can count on each other, come what may. And when teammates respect each other, trust each other, and are loyal to each other, there's no limit to what they can accomplish.

A number of years ago, the Dallas Mavericks played the Magic in Orlando. Before the game, I talked to Bob Ortegel, the broadcast voice of the Mavericks. Bob's eyes were alight with excitement as he shared an insight he had recently discovered. "Pat!" Bob said. "I've had a great revelation! I've finally figured out basketball!"

"Oh? What do you mean?"

"Pat, if I have the ball and I pass it to you, I trust you to pass it back to me if I'm more open than you are."

"And?"

"That's it! That's all there is to basketball!"

Then he walked away. I know I must have looked completely befuddled by Bob's "great revelation"—but as I pondered what he had said, I realized he was right. He had just broken the game of basketball down to its purest essence: It's a game of respect, trust, and loyalty. If teammates respect each other, they play in such a way that they learn to trust each other with the ball, and that leads to loyalty of one teammate to another, so that the players can play unselfishly, always giving the ball to the player with the open shot. That is why teams with the greatest mutual respect, trust, and loyalty have the best chance of winning.

Then, loyalty leads to love. We've talked about unconditional love in previous chapters, and we're going to talk about it one more time—it's *that* important. One of the greatest coaches of all time, Vince Lombardi, put it this way in a conversation over dinner with industrialist Lee Iacocca: "If you're going to play together as a team, you've got to care for one another. You've got to love each other. Each player has to be thinking about the next guy and saying to himself: 'If I don't block that man, my teammate's going to get his legs broken. I have to do my job well so that my teammates can do theirs.' The difference between mediocrity and greatness is the feeling these guys have for each other."[111]

When teammates respect each other, when they've learned to trust each other, when they have demonstrated their loyalty to each other through the good times and the hard times, what else can they feel for each other but love? And love between teammates leads to friendships that last a lifetime.

David Halberstam's *The Teammates: A Portrait of a Friendship* tells the story of four legendary teammates from the 1940s Boston Red Sox—Ted Williams, Dominic DiMaggio, Bobby Doerr, and Johnny Pesky. It's a book that tugs at the heart, because it tells the story of how these four teammates respected each other, trusted each other, demonstrated loyalty to each other, and ultimately loved each other as lifelong friends.

(A personal aside: I used to go to the Hitters Hall of Fame events when Ted Williams was living. On one occasion, all four of those great Red Sox teammates—Williams, DiMaggio, Doerr, and Pesky—were in attendance and in good health. They were lined up to have their picture taken. As the photographer prepared to snap the picture, I jumped into the shot, as if I were one of their long-lost teammates. The photographer snapped the picture—and I have that photo framed on the wall of my library at home.)

In his book, David Halberstam writes about how Johnny Pesky and Dom DiMaggio went to visit Ted Williams in Florida as he was sick and dying. They found Ted to be a mere wisp of his former self, weighing only 130 pounds and living out his final days in a wheelchair. Halberstam writes:

> They visited with Ted for two days, two visits a day, each one not too long, because he needed his naps. On the last visit, Dominic suddenly said, "Teddy, I'm going to sing you a song." It was an Italian love song,

the story of two men who were best friends, one of whom was in love with a girl. But he was afraid to tell her, so he did it through his friend, who stole her away. "I Love Her, but I Don't Know How to Tell Her," Dominic called it. Then Dominic began to sing and the house was filled with the sound of his beautiful baritone voice. Ted loved it, he started clapping, and so Dominic sang it again, and Ted clapped again. Then Dominic sang "Me and My Shadow" for him. "Dommy, Dommy, you did really well," Ted said when he finished.[112]

Fifty years had passed since Ted Williams and Dom DiMaggio were Red Sox teammates, yet they were still friends—the kind of friends who are there for you and who'd even sing to you in your final days.

Halberstam goes on to tell how Dom DiMaggio, long after his retirement from baseball, became a successful business owner with his own manufacturing company. DiMaggio learned that his old teammate, Johnny Pesky, was still working in a minor capacity for the Red Sox organization, but was woefully underpaid. So DiMaggio contacted Pesky and offered him a job with his company at a considerable increase in salary. Though Pesky was grateful for the offer, he turned it down. "Dom, I couldn't love my own brothers more than I love you, and I want to thank you, but I am a baseball man, and it's all I'll ever be. It's all I know. I'll wear the uniform until I die, and then they'll probably have to cut it off me."[113]

These teammates, decades after they had played together on the Red Sox, were not ashamed to say "I love you" to each other. They were friends. They cared about each other. They loved each other to the end of their days.

Respect leads to trust. Trust leads to loyalty. Loyalty leads to love. And the love between teammates leads to friendships that cannot be broken except by death itself. Wouldn't you like to have friendships built on mutual respect, on love for the game, and on love for each other? Wouldn't you like to have friendships that would last until you breathe your last breath?

You can. It all begins with respect. When you live out respect for the game and respect for your teammates, you're well on your way to becoming the best teammate anybody ever had. The Ultimate Teammate is a teammate who demonstrates respect—and earns it for life.

15

PLAY YOUR
ROLE

"I am a member of a team, and I rely on the team, I defer to it and sacrifice for it, because the team, not the individual, is the ultimate champion."

—Retired Soccer Player Mia Hamm

Benis Arapovic/Hemera/Thinkstock

After having coached Jameer Nelson for five seasons with the Magic, Stan Van Gundy told me, "Jameer is one of those rare players who's both a great individual performer and a great team player. It's a lot easier to find great performers than it is to find great teammates who fit in well and play their roles. Good team chemistry is the result of players who work well together. It's a rare thing—and Jameer has it."

The Magic's current head coach, Jacque Vaughn, has been Jameer's coach for two years. Jacque told me: "Jameer Nelson is a great teammate because of his willingness to be unselfish. He is committed to setting aside his own interests to do whatever is best for the team. Being a good teammate means communicating through words and example. It's not easy to be a good teammate. It takes the rare ability to die to yourself every day, the ability to exterminate your own ego so that you can serve a greater cause. A great teammate stays engaged even when he's not playing, so that he'll be ready to perform when his turn comes."

If you want to be the best teammate anybody has ever had, you've got to know your role and play your role. Whether you are a starter or the guy at the end of the bench, you've got to prepare every day as if a championship season is riding on your shoulders. Whether or not you expect to see any playing time, you've got to keep your head in the game and your adrenalin pumping so you'll be ready when the coach calls your number.

Michael Jordan described the crucial importance of knowing and playing your role when he talked about his glory days with the Chicago Bulls: "When we started winning championships, there was an understanding among all twelve players about what our roles were. We knew we had responsibilities and we knew our capabilities. Those were the kinds of things we had to understand and accept if we were going to win championships."[114]

And Bill Russell, the centerpiece of the Celtics dynasty of the late 1950s and 1960s, wrote in his autobiography: "I wanted to lead the league in rebounding. Cousy wanted to lead the league in assists. Sharman wanted to lead the league in free-throw percentage. Heinsohn wanted to lead the league in field goals taken. ... The good thing about it was that no two Celtics had the same goals, and nobody was trying to play the wrong role."[115]

If everybody on the team is trying to do play the same role and achieve the same goals, you don't have a team. Every successful team consists of a group of diverse players in diverse roles pursuing diverse individual goals and functions, but all unified on the overarching team goal of winning the game, winning the championship. All great teams are made of players who know their roles and play their roles in order to achieve a unity of purpose.

The Astonishing Power of Role Players

Another Celtics legend, Larry Bird, played basketball with the Indiana State University Sycamores for three years in the late 1970s. Bird led the Sycamores to their first NCAA tournament in school history, including the historic championship game against Michigan State in 1979. The game achieved the highest-ever TV ratings for any college basketball game because of the exciting match-up between Larry Bird and point guard Magic Johnson of the Michigan State Spartans.

Though Magic and the Spartans won the championship, Larry Bird earned many honors and awards that season, including the Naismith College Player of the Year Award. Bird led Indiana State to an 81-13 record during his college career, and went on to play for the Boston Celtics in the NBA. Magic Johnson went on to play for the Los Angeles Lakers, and the Bird-Magic rivalry that began in the NCAA continued on throughout their NBA careers.

Larry Bird looked back on his days playing for Indiana State, and he concluded that the key to the team's success was that every player knew his role and played it. "We didn't have a lot of NBA talent on our team," he said, "but we were a team. When you have a team of guys who know their roles and stick to their roles, you can't get any better than that. Yeah, I was the focal point, and I was the one scoring the points and getting the rebounds, but if it wasn't for these other four guys with me, it would have never worked."[116]

Broadcaster Dick Vitale, who coached college basketball at Rutgers and the University of Detroit, has a simple explanation for why role players are so important in the game of basketball. "A basketball team is only five players, man," he said. "If you come up with a superstar and find four others who know their roles, you can go out and shock a lot of people. You don't need the numbers the way you do in football."[117]

Barbara Stevens, the head women's basketball coach of the Bentley University Falcons in Waltham, Massachusetts, can attest to the truth of Dick Vitale's claim: a team really can create shockwaves when *all* the players—especially the ones who are *not* superstars—know and play their roles. Coach Stevens told me this story about the importance of playing your role:

> Some years ago, we had a player named Eileen Prendergast. As a freshman, Eileen was the 14th player on a 14-player team. She rarely entered a game, and usually only for mop-up duty. Yet Eileen made a big impression on me and her teammates through her passion for the game and her work ethic. She was the first one in the gym and the last

to leave. She constantly asked our coaching staff to work with her and help her improve. Our coaches loved her enthusiasm, even though we never thought she'd be a major contributor to our program.

As a sophomore, Eileen moved up the depth chart a bit, though her skills were still lacking. Offensively, she tended to play too fast and out of control. Her ball handling and shooting were weak. But Eileen was quick and aggressive, and her mental toughness kept her going when everyone else was spent. She never quit, and never stopped working on her game.

One night after practice during Eileen's sophomore year, I was at my desk and I heard a knock at my office door. There was Eileen. She looked distressed. "Coach," she said, "I'm trying so hard every day. I know where I stand on the team, but I want you to know that if you ever need me, I'll be ready."

I thanked Eileen and urged her to keep working hard. But I knew her skills were still lacking, and I doubted there'd be a time when we'd desperately need her.

The following season, she continued to improve, and she made a niche for herself as the team's defensive specialist. She was assigned to cover the opponent's point guard and her aggressiveness disrupted many of our opponents' offenses. She had been a walk-on her first two years, but with her increased role, Eileen earned a scholarship for her senior season. As a sign of respect for all she had contributed to the team, her teammates elected her co-captain.

In Eileen's senior year, we approached the season ranked as the pre-season number-one team in the nation in NCAA Division II. We were optimistic about our chances, because we had key players returning from a team that had gone 33 and 3 the previous year and had advanced to the Final Four. There were four seniors on the team: Missy Wolfe, a four-year starter at point guard, one of the best in our conference; Cathy Sterner, a six-foot finesse forward who was a key reserve in the frontcourt; Tracie Seymour, an athletic wing guard with tremendous skills; and Eileen Prendergast, our plucky reserve guard with limited offensive ability but great defensive tenacity.

As the season began, we tore through our schedule and dominated the opposition. By early January, the Bentley Falcons were 10 and 0. Next on the schedule was our Northeast Ten rival, St. Anselm College. The Falcons took control of the game early and were rolling toward another victory. But, with less than 10 minutes to play, the unthinkable happened: Missy Wolfe, our co-captain and charismatic leader, went down with a knee injury (it ultimately ended her career).

In that moment, it looked like our dream season was over. Without Missy, our hopes for a national championship appeared dashed. In fact, we doubted we'd be able to win our conference. Though we won the game against St. Anselm, the rest of our schedule was shrouded in gloom and uncertainty.

The day after that fateful game, we held a light shooting practice. I walked around and spoke with each player, trying to be positive and encouraging. But I knew my words rang hollow. Everyone felt as bad as I did about Missy—her injury dominated our thoughts. How could we win without her?

I asked our junior All-American forward, Kim Penwell, if she could play some point guard until we got Missy's back-up ready. She said, "Coach, I'll play any role you want me to play." She was having a fantastic season at forward, yet I was asking her to change to a position she'd never played before. But Kim didn't complain. She gave me a look that radiated confidence and said, "Don't worry, Coach. We're going to be okay."

As Kim and I talked, Eileen stood nearby, listening intently. She had a look in her eye that told me all I wanted to know—she was every bit as confident and optimistic as Kim was. The look on her face was absolutely fearless.

I said, "Eileen do you remember when you came to my office and said, 'Coach, if you ever need me, I'll be ready'? Well, Eileen, I need you right now."

So we prepared for our next game. Led by Kim and Eileen and senior Tracie Seymour, the Bentley Falcons amazed everyone, including their coach! They kept right on winning, taking the next 21 games in a row. We advanced to our fourth consecutive appearance in the NCAA Division II Final Four. Bentley's record going into the last weekend of the season was 31 and 0.

We didn't reach our goal of a national championship, but our players did exemplify the essence of sport and competition. Each of our players had a role to play, and each understood and accepted that role and did what needed to be done. They sacrificed, adapted to new roles, and overcame the crisis of Missy's injury in order to achieve greatness. They taught me more than I could ever teach them, because they were able to summon the confidence I lacked.

In short, they truly became a *team*. And who would have thought, during Eileen Prendergast's freshman year, that she—the 14th player on a 14-player team—would be the heart and soul of that team?"

The Best Lug Nut Ever

When I hear the term *role player*, I often think of Donald Royal, a role player with the Orlando Magic in the 1990s. Donald had known some struggles in his pro career. After graduating from Notre Dame, he played for Pensacola and Cedar Rapids in the minor league Continental Basketball Association. He moved up briefly to the NBA, playing for the Minnesota Timberwolves, then played for a season with the Maccabi Tel Aviv (Israel) basketball club, then back to the CBA and a season with the Tri-City, Washington, Chinook, then a season with the San Antonio Spurs, after which he settled in with the Magic for a few seasons.

Donald Royal played a supporting role to such stars as Shaquille O'Neal, Penny Hardaway, and Horace Grant, and received relatively little attention from the media and the fans. Yet, because he was not a razzle-dazzle player like Shaq, Penny, or Horace, he added some key strengths to our game. Royal was a strong defensive player and a dependable rebounder, so he was always in position as a back-screen for the Shaq Attack.

"I'm a role player," he said in an interview with *The Sporting News*. "It's no big deal for me not to score a lot. I'm a guy who's out there to do the little things."[118] One of the "little things" he did so well was making free throws. He drained 80 percent of his shots from the line. He was also an excellent outside shooter, often shocking our opponents with 18-foot shots. Though Donald Royal was never a star, he was a key component of our team. He knew his role, he played it to the hilt, and his contributions often spelled the difference between winning and losing.

There are no unimportant teammates. Even if you are not a superstar, even if you are a role player, you can be the best teammate anybody has ever had. All you have to do is make sure that you are always prepared to step in, work hard, and play your role. Whether you are a starter or a sub, know your role and play your role to the hilt. Be the best-prepared player anyone could be, and someday you'll get your chance to prove yourself.

Coach John Wooden believed that every player had an important, irreplaceable role to play on the team. He had a powerful analogy he used to get this concept across to his players—the analogy of a finely tuned sports car. He explained:

> I told players at UCLA that we, as a team, are like a powerful car. Maybe a Bill Walton or Kareem Abdul-Jabbar … is the big engine, but if one wheel is flat, we're going no place. And if we have brand-new tires but the lug nuts are missing, the wheels come off. What good is a powerful engine now? It's no good at all.

A lug nut may seem like a little thing, but it's not. There's a role that each and every one of us must play. We may aspire to what we consider to be a larger role, or a more important role, but we cannot achieve that until we show that we are able to fulfill the role we are assigned. It's these little things that make the big things happen. ...

Of course, when I told the players about their roles and the car with the powerful engine, new tires, and tight lug nuts, I also reminded them the car needed a driver behind the wheel or it would just go around in circles or smash into a tree.

I told them the driver was me.[119]

So whether you are an engine or a lug nut on your team, know your role and play your role. There are no unimportant roles. A lug nut may seem like a little thing, and lug nuts may only cost 49 cents apiece at Pep Boys®, but just try driving your car without them and see how far you get. If you are a lug nut on your team, make sure you are a snug-fitting lug nut and that you keep your team's wheels fastened on.

Heightened Group Consciousness

Phil Jackson, who coached the Chicago Bulls and the Los Angeles Lakers to a combined total of 11 NBA championships, coined a term for the team mindset that Coach Wooden described: "heightened group consciousness." He wrote:

The day I took over the Bulls, I vowed to create an environment based on ... principles of selflessness and compassion. ... I knew that the only way to win consistently was to give everybody—from the stars to the number twelve player on the bench—a vital role on the team, and inspire them to be acutely aware of what was happening, even when the spotlight was on somebody else. More than anything, I wanted to build a team that would blend individual talent with a heightened group consciousness.[120]

If you want to be the best teammate anybody has ever had, you must immerse your own personal ego into that heightened group consciousness. You must think team, not self. You must think unity, not individual achievement.

Talent is vitally important on any team—but many talented players forget the importance of teamwork and chemistry. Selfishness and arrogance can destroy a team. Players who think "me," not "we," are chemistry-killers. They put themselves above the team. What good does all your talent do you if you waste it all on your own ego instead of on playing your role and elevating your team?

To be the Ultimate Teammate, set your ego aside, put your teammates above yourself, maintain a well-balanced team chemistry, and *play your role*. Instead of trying to lead the league in arrogance, try leading the league in humility and in supporting your teammates. If you know your role and play your role, you'll shock a lot of people and win a lot of games.

EPILOGUE
A FINAL CHALLENGE

By now, you've probably figured out that the 15 principles discussed in this book do not stand in isolation from each other. They are all interconnected. They fit together and build on each other. You have to be teachable, coachable, and humble in order to play your role. You have to maintain a consistent, positive attitude in order to empower others. You have to be 100 percent committed in order to persevere through adversity, in order to not quit.

Following, for your review, are the 15 keys to becoming the best teammate anybody has ever had:

1. Empower others—be an encourager to your teammates.
2. Work hard—be an example of a strong work ethic to your teammates.
3. Maintain a consistent, positive attitude—be a motivator to your teammates.
4. Be a character person—live as a role model to your teammates.
5. Be responsible—make yourself accountable to your teammates.
6. Be a leader—summon the best from your teammates.
7. Be teachable and coachable—focus on continuous growth and maturity.
8. Hit the books—maintain your eligibility for the sake of your teammates.
9. Be fully prepared—be ready when your number is called.
10. Be 100 percent committed—be a player your teammates can count on.
11. Don't quit—inspire your teammates to keep fighting, no matter what.
12. Be passionate—energize and excite your teammates.
13. Stay humble—be a servant to your teammates.
14. Respect your teammates—give them the consideration they're due.
15. Play your role—put the team ahead of self.

Whatever your sport, whether you compete at the high school, college, or professional level, if you can become a teammate who exemplifies all of these traits, you'll be the best teammate anybody ever had. And just imagine if everyone on your team became an Ultimate Teammate! How far could your team go? What heights might your team reach?

So what follows is my challenge to you—and to all of your teammates: Study these 15 principles. Build them into your life. Live them out in the locker room, on the practice field, and on the field of competition. Live them out throughout the season and even in the off-season. Be the best teammate anybody ever had—then watch what happens.

After all, if your team consists of nothing but Ultimate Teammates, what else could it be but the Ultimate Team!

ENDNOTES

1. Atlantic 10. (2011). Jameer Nelson Feature—35th Anniversary [YouTube video]. Transcribed by the author. Available from http://www.youtube.com/watch?v=lOhRqExlw9U.

2. Tiplady, R. (2003). *One world or many? The impact of globalisation on mission*. Pasadena, CA: William Carey Library, 43.

3. Soderquist, D. (2005). *Live, learn, lead to make a difference*. Nashville, TN: Thomas Nelson, 129.

4. Fellowship of Christian Athletes. (2008). *Serving: True champions know that success takes sacrifice*. Ventura, CA: Regal Books, 147.

5. Schmitz, B. (2009). Great "D" and big shots by VC make for a happy Van Gundy," *Orlando Sentinel*, November 21, 2009, http://articles.orlandosentinel.com/2009-11-21/sports/0911210017_1_stan-van-gundy-cleveland-cavs-dwight-howard.

6. Coughlin, T., and Fisher, D. (2013). *Earn the right to win: How success in any field starts with superior preparation*. New York: Portfolio/Penguin.

7. Bryant, H. (2010). *The last hero: A life of Henry Aaron*. New York: Pantheon, 330.

8. Miller, J.A., and Shales, T. (2011). *Those guys have all the fun: Inside the world of ESPN*. New York: Hachette, 758–759.

9. Stratton, W.K. (2012). *Floyd Patterson: The fighting life of boxing's invisible champion*. New York: Houghton Mifflin Harcourt, 181.

10. Alvey, R. (2010). From one big leaguer to another. iLife Journey blog, October 14, 2010, http://ilifejourney.wordpress.com/tag/orel-hershiser/.

11. Bodley, H. (2005). New hall of famers frustrated by lack of respect for game. *USA Today*, July 31, 2005, http://usatoday30.usatoday.com/sports/baseball/columnist/bodley/2005-07-31-bodley-hall_x.htm.

12. Wooden, J., and Jamison, S. (2009). *Coach Wooden's leadership game plan for success: 12 lessons for extraordinary performance and personal excellence*. New York: McGraw Hill Professional, 135.

13. Russell, B., and Steinberg, A. (2009). *Red and me: My coach, my lifelong friend*. New York: HarperCollins, 55.

14. Simon, R.J. (1997). *In the golden land: A century of Russian and Soviet Jewish immigration in America*. Westport, CT: Praeger Publishers, 119.

15. Parker, S. (2005). *212: The extra degree*. Dallas, TX: Walk the Talk, 1–2.

16. Corbett, J. (2009). Everything but the title: Drew Brees is crashing the QB party," *USA Today*, October 3, 2009, http://usatoday30.usatoday.com/sports/football/nfl/saints/2009-10-01-drew-brees-cover_N.htm.

17. Ibid.

18. Gould, S.J., and Halberstam, D. (2003). *Triumph and tragedy in Mudville: A lifelong passion for baseball.* New York: W.W. Norton, 321.

19. English, A. (2010). Former Florida star quarterback Tim Tebow drafted in first round by Denver Broncos. *Tampa Bay Times*, April 22, 2010, http://www.tampabay.com/sports/football/bucs/former-florida-star-quarterback-tim-tebow-drafted-in-first-round-by-denver/1089686.

20. Tracy, B. (2004). *Million dollar habits: Proven power practices to double and triple your income.* Irvine, CA: Entrepreneur Media, 93–94.

21. Kramer, J., and Schaap, D. (2011). *Instant replay: The Green Bay diary of Jerry Kramer.* New York: Anchor Books, 36.

22. District 4 Big League. (n.d.). Stepping up to the plate. Retrieved March 25, 2014 from http://www.d4bigleague.com/custpage.php?cid=84.

23. King, C., and King, H.T. (2006). *Don't play for the tie: Bear Bryant on life.* Nashville: Rutledge Hill Press, 54.

24. Ibid., 98.

25. Investor's Business Daily. (2004). *Sports Leaders & Success: 55 Top Sports Leaders & How They Achieved Greatness.* New York: McGraw-Hill, 20–21.

26. McCallum, J. (2004). Uh-kay, you have a 70-year-old coach named Hubie: Now what does that mean? *Sports Illustrated*, March 8, 2004, http://sportsillustrated.cnn.com/vault/article/magazine/MAG1031352/1/index.htm.

27. Dickson, P. (2009). *The Dickson baseball dictionary* (3rd ed.). New York: Norton, 198.

28. Saint Joseph's University Hawks. (2004). Jameer Nelson makes homecoming to Philadelphia. November 15, 2004, http://www.sjuhawks.com/ViewArticle.dbml?SPSID=750595&SPID=127360&DB_OEM_ID=31200&ATCLID=208726346.

29. Corcoran, D. (2011). *Induction day at Cooperstown: A history of the Baseball Hall of Fame ceremony.* Jefferson, NC: McFarland, 215.

30. Air Force Journal of Logistics. (2001). *Quotes for the Air Force Logistician.* Maxwell AFB, AL: Air Force Logistics Management Agency 60.

31. Thompson, R. (2000). Living the right life. *The Morning Smile*, July 4, 2000, http://groups.yahoo.com/neo/groups/TheMorningSmile/conversations/topics/382?l=1.

32. Waitley, D. (1980). *The winner's edge: How to develop the critical attitude for success.* New York: Times Books.

33. Frankl, V.E. (1984). *Man's search for meaning.* New York: Simon & Schuster, 75.

34. Roca, H. and Silverglade, B. (2006). *The Gleason's Gym total body boxing workout for women.* New York: Simon & Schuster, 9.

35. Williams, P. (1998). *Go for the Magic.* Nashville, TN: Thomas Nelson, 115.

36. Farley, K.L., and Curry, S.M. (1994). *Get motivated! Daily psych-ups.* New York: Simon & Schuster, entry for January 14.

37. Buyer, P. (2013). *3 strategies for developing EFFORT in your students and employees.* February 3, 2013, http://www.paulbuyer.com/3-strategies-for-developing-effort-in-your-student-and-employees.

38. Townsend, C. (n.d.). Sports psychology—How does a champion swimmer think? Mind training tips for swimmers. About.com Swimming. Retrieved from http://swimming.about.com/od/swimmingmindtrainingtips/qt/How-Does-A-Champion-Swimmer-Think.htm.

39. Wooden, J., and Carty, J. (2009). *Coach Wooden's pyramid of success: Building blocks for a better life.* Ventura, CA: Regal Books, 130.

40. Wooden, J. (2004). *My personal best: Life lessons from an all-American journey.* New York: McGraw-Hill Professional, 116.

41. Lombardi, V. Jr. (2012). *Lombardi: Rules and lessons on what it takes to be #1.* New York: McGraw-Hill Professional, 7–8.

42. Lombardi, V. Jr. (2002). *The essential Vince Lombardi: Words & wisdom to motivate, inspire, and win.* New York: McGraw-Hill, 177.

43. Ibid., 176.

44. King, C., and King, H.T. (2006). *Don't play for the tie: Bear Bryant on life.* Nashville, TN: Rutledge Hill Press, 95.

45. Selleck, G.A. (1999). *Court sense: The invisible edge in basketball and life.* Lanham, MD: Rowman & Littlefield, 104.

46. Coughlin, T., and Fisher, D. (2013). *Earn the right to win: How success in any field starts with superior preparation.* New York: Penguin.

47. Landry, T., and Lewis, G.A. (1990). *Tom Landry: An autobiography.* Grand Rapids, MI: Zondervan, 292.

48. John, B. (2000). *Landry: The legend and the legacy.* Nashville, TN: Thomas Nelson, 221.

49. Maraniss, D. (1999). *When pride still mattered: A life of Vince Lombardi.* New York: Simon & Schuster.

50. Ewert, J. (2007). A royal risk. *Sharing the Victory,* http://archives.fca.org/vsItemDisplay.lsp?method=display&objectid=0B6089DD-07C1-4E41-AEE59F2F35B1C94F.

51. Ruth, G.H. "Babe." (1948). The kids can't take it if we don't give it! *Guideposts,* October 1948. Retrieved from http://www.catholicjournal.us/2013/06/02/the-kids-cant-take-it-if-we-dont-give-it/.

52. Russell, B, and Falkner, D. (2001). *Russell rules: 11 lessons on leadership from the twentieth century's greatest winner.* New York: New American Library, 155.

53. Summitt, P. (1998). *Reach for the summit.* New York: Broadway, 29.

54. Vincent, F. (2010). *It's what's inside the lines that counts: Baseball stars of the 1970s and 1980s talk about the game they loved.* New York: Simon & Schuster, 241, 250–251.

55. Gold, E. (2007). *Bear's boys: 36 men whose lives were changed by coach Paul Bryant.* Nashville, TN: Thomas Nelson, 147.

56. Watts, J.C. Jr. (2002). *What color is a conservative?* New York: HarperCollins, 34.

57. Krzyzewski, M., and Phillips, D.T. (2000). *Leading with the heart: Coach K's successful strategies for basketball, business, and life.* New York: Warner Books, 40–42.

58. Gruden, J., and Carucci, V. (2003). *Do You Love Football?! Winning With Heart, Passion, & Not Much Sleep.* New York: HarperCollins, 89.

59. Paulson, T.L. (2010). *The optimism advantage: 50 simple truths to transform your attitudes and actions into results.* Hoboken, NJ: Wiley, 10.

60. Russell, B., and Falkner, D. (2001). *Russell rules: 11 lessons on leadership from the 20th century's greatest winner.* New York: New American Library, 192.

61. Robinson, E., and Lapchick, R. (1999). *Never before, never again: The stirring autobiography of Eddie Robinson, the winningest coach in the history of college football.* New York: St. Martin's Press, 114.

62. Lombardi, V. Jr. (2001). *What it takes to be #1: Vince Lombardi on leadership.* New York: McGraw-Hill, 91.

63. Detroit News. (2001). *They earned their stripes: The Detroit Tigers' all-time team.* Champaign, IL: Sports Publishing, Inc., 28.

64. Krzyzewski, M. (2006). Quotes, CoachK.com, September 2006, http://coachk.com/coach-k-media/quotes.

65. Curry, B. Love & acceptance. Video clip viewed and transcribed at https://www.youtube.com/watch?v=g2OrpmqEDRw&noredirect=1.

66. Frazier, W., and Markowitz, D. (2006). *The game within the game* (New York: Hyperion, 16–17.

67. Dunnavant, K. (2011). *Bart Starr and the rise of the National Football League.* New York: St. Martin's, 31.

68. Schleier, C. (2002). Mike Krzyzewski wins by valuing teamwork strategy for success. *Investor's Business Daily*, April 11, 2002, http://www.accessmylibrary.com/article-1G1-106002907/mike-krzyzewski-wins-valuing.html.

69. Ramsay, J. (2002). My secrets to NBA head coaching success. ESPN.com: NBA, September 19, 2002; http://sports.espn.go.com/nba/columns/story?columnist=ramsay_drjack&id=1434127.

70. Jackson, P., and Delahanty, H. (1995). *Sacred hoops: Spiritual lessons of a hardwood warrior.* New York: Hyperion, 101.

71. Turak, A. (2011). Are you coachable? The five steps to coachability. *Forbes*, September 30, 2011, http://www.forbes.com/sites/augustturak/2011/09/30/are-you-coachable-the-five-steps-to-coachability/.

72. Wendleton, K. (2014). *Mastering the job interview and winning the money game.* Boston, MA: Cengage, 176.

73. Wooden, J., and Jamison, S. (1997). *Wooden: A lifetime of observations and reflections on and off the court.* Chicago: Contemporary Books, 133.

74. Wooden, J., and Jamison, S. (2006). *The essential Wooden: A lifetime of lessons on leaders and leadership.* New York: McGraw-Hill, 65.

75. Ibid., 70–71.

76. Nater, S. and Gallimore, R. (2005). *You haven't taught until they have learned: John Wooden's teaching principles and practices.* Morgantown, WV: Fitness Information Technology, 69.

77. Ibid., 69–70.

78. Miller, S.L. (2009). *Why teams win: 9 keys to success in business, sport, and beyond.* Mississauga, Ontario: John Wiley & Sons Canada, 117.

79. Lombardi, V. Jr. (2001). *What it takes to be #1: Vince Lombardi on leadership.* New York: McGraw-Hill, 91.

80. Veloskey, K.M. (2010). Football great returning to Janesville. October 15, 2010, http://gazettextra.com/apps/pbcs.dll/article?avis=JG&date=20101015&category=ARTICLES&lopenr=310159999&Ref=AR&print.

81. Williams, P., and Hussar, K. (2011). *The ultimate handbook of motivational quote for coaches and leaders.* Monterey, CA: Coaches Choice, 276.

82. Carchidi, S. (2006). B*ill Campbell: The voice of Philadelphia sports.* Moorestown, NJ: Middle Atlantic Press, 85.

83. Bettinger, J., and Bettinger, J.S. (2007). *The book of Bowden: Words of wisdom, faith, and motivation by and about Bobby Bowden.* Lanham, MD: Rowman & Littlefield, 122.

84. Mitchell, F. (1987). Gooden shows Cubs he's in control again. *Chicago Tribune,* June 26, 1987, http://articles.chicagotribune.com/1987-06-26/sports/8702160951_1_smithers-clinic-mookie-wilson-cubs.

85. Leusner, J. (1996). Smith: Move to drugs was "stupidity." *Orlando Sentinel,* June 16, 1996, http://articles.orlandosentinel.com/1996-06-16/news/9606150647_1_smith-powder-cocaine-crack.

86. Johnson, A., and Johnson, R.S. (2008). *Aspire higher.* New York: HarperCollins, 46.

87. Wooden, J., and Carty, J. (2005). *Coach Wooden's pyramid of success playbook: Applying the pyramid of success to your life.* Ventura, CA: Regal, 13.

88. Curry, B. (2008). *Ten men you meet in the huddle: Lessons from a football life.* New York: ESPN Books, 236–237, 239.

89. Indianapolis Star News. (1999). *Larry Bird: An Indiana legend.* Champaign, IL: Sports Publishing, 93.

90. King, P. (2005). T.O.'s Super Bowl saga can't compare to Youngblood's. *Sports Illustrated,* January 31, 2005, http://sportsillustrated.cnn.com/2005/writers/peter_king/01/30/mmqb.sboffweek.ii/index.html.

91. Drehs, W. (2003). Wait over for Hall-bound Youngblood. November 19, 2003, Retrieved March 14 2014 from http://espn.go.com/classic/s/2001/0127/1044351.html; Harris, L. What we're about. The Ed Block Courage Award, http://www.edblock.org/about.htm; Danyluk, T. and Zimmerman, P. (2005). *The super '70s: Memories from pro football's greatest era.* Chicago: Mad Uke Publishing, 213.

92. MacCambridge, M. (2005). *America's game: The epic story of how pro football captured a nation.* New York: Anchor Books, 447.

93. Blaylock, M. (2000). *The right way to win: How athletes can place god first in their hearts.* Chicago: Moody Press, 69.

94. Castro, T. (2002). *Mickey Mantle: America's prodigal son.* Washington: Potomac Books, 99–100.

95. Russell, A. (1998). *A Steeler odyssey*. Champaign, IL: Sports Publishing, 153–154; Kilduff, M. (2001). Passion play: Athletes describe their love for playing sports. Sporting News, August 27, 2001, Retrieved from http://findarticles.com/p/articles/mi_m1208/is_35_225/ai_77811426.

96. Krzyzewski, M., and Spatola, J.K. (2006). *Beyond basketball: Coach K's keywords for success*. New York: Warner Business Books, 121.

97. Price, S.L. (2002). Coach Chucky. *Sports Illustrated*, September 9, 2002, http://sportsillustrated.cnn.com/vault/article/magazine/MAG1026703/6/index.htm.

98. Papanek, J. (1980). A chess game with soul. *Sports Illustrated*, October 20, 1980, http://sportsillustrated.cnn.com/vault/article/magazine/MAG1123871/2/index.htm.

99. Starkey, B. (2009). The great ones love to practice, prepare. September 7, 2009, http://hoopthoughts.blogspot.com/2009/09/great-ones-love-to-practice-prepare.html.

100. Bowden, B., and Bowden, S. (2001). *The Bowden way: 50 years of leadership wisdom*. Atlanta: Longstreet Press, 173.

101. Ibid., 180–181.

102. Spiewak, P. (2010). Game day feature: Jameer Nelson. St. Joseph's University Hawks, SJUHawks.com, February 9, 2010, http://www.sjuhawks.com/ViewArticle.dbml?SPSID=750595&SPID=127360&DB_OEM_ID=31200&ATCLID=208724172.

103. O'Connell, J. (1995). "Wizard of Westwood" holds dreams of UCLA's glorious past. *Park City Daily News*, March 29, 1995, 1B–2B.

104. Fox Sports and Current Video. (2013). Jameer Nelson on hazing [embedded video]. Transcribed by the authors. Retrieved from http://video.us.msn.com/watch/video/jameer-nelson-on-hazing/12lzh3p8?cpkey=b07fedaf-f23d-4564-8349-c85c617ba144%257c%257c%257c%257c.

105. Johnson, N.L. (2003). *The John Wooden pyramid of success: The authorized biography*. Los Angeles: Cool Titles, 122–123.

106. Bodley, H. (2005). New hall of famers frustrated by lack of respect for game. *USA Today*, July 31, 2005, http://usatoday30.usatoday.com/sports/baseball/columnist/bodley/2005-07-31-bodley-hall_x.htm.

107. Sandberg, R. (2005). Respect the game. Yahoo Sports, August 1, 2005, http://sports.yahoo.com/mlb/news?slug=rs-speech080105.

108. Livingstone, S. (2002). Gardenhire teaches respect for the game. *USA Today Baseball Weekly*, May 14, 2002, Retrieved from http://www.usatoday.com/sports/bbw/2002-05-15/extra.htm.

109. Araton, H. (2001). Sports of the times; Jeter lays off his pal's bait, saying plenty. *New York Times*, March 6, 2001, Retrieved March 25, 2014 from http://www.nytimes.com/2001/03/06/sports/sports-of-the-times-jeter-lays-off-his-pal-s-bait-saying-plenty.html.

110. Miller, K.L., and Muller, J. (1998). Jurgen Schrempp: The Auto Baron. *BusinessWeek*, November 16, 1998, Retrieved March 25, 2014 from http://www.businessweek.com/1998/46/b3604044.htm.

111. Iacocca, L., and Novak, W. (1984). *Iacocca: An autobiography*. New York: Bantam Dell, 60.

112. Halberstam, D. (2003). *The teammates: A portrait of a friendship*. New York: Hyperion, 197.

113. Ibid., 47–48.

114. Prentice-Hall. (1999). *Workplace writing*. Upper Saddle River, NJ: Prentice Hall, 85.

115. Russell, B., and Branch, T. (1979). *Second wind: The memoirs of an opinionated man*. New York: Random House, 124.

116. NCAA Student-Athlete Name & Likeness Licensing Litigation. C 09-01967 CW, 44. (United States District Court, Northern District of California, Oakland Division, filed July 18, 2013). Retrieved from http://www.scribd.com/doc/154771300/Ncaa.

117. Vitale, D. (2003). *Dick Vitale's living a dream: Reflections on 25 years sitting in the best seats in the house*. Champaign, IL: Sports Publishing, 145–146.

118. Heller, B. (1995). The fifth man. *The Sporting News*, January 23, 1995, 33.

119. Wooden, J., and S. Jamison. (1997). *Wooden: A lifetime of observations and reflections on and off the court*. Chicago: Contemporary Books, 75–76.

120. Jackson, P., and Delehanty, H. (2006). *Sacred hoops: Spiritual lessons of a hardwood warrior*. New York: Hyperion, 4.

ABOUT THE
AUTHOR

Pat Williams is the senior vice president of the NBA's Orlando Magic. As one of America's top motivational, inspirational, and humorous speakers, he has addressed thousands of executives in organizations ranging from Fortune 500 companies and national associations to universities and nonprofits. Clients include Allstate, American Express, Cisco, Coca-Cola, Disney, Honeywell, IBM, ING, Lockheed Martin, Nike, PriceWaterhouseCoopers, and Tyson Foods to name a few. Pat is also the author of over 90 books.

Pat served for seven years in the United States Army, spent seven years in the Philadelphia Phillies organization—two as a Minor League catcher and five in the front office—and has also spent three years in the Minnesota Twins organization. Since 1968, he has been in the NBA as general manager for teams in Chicago, Atlanta, and Philadelphia—including the 1983 World Champion 76ers—and now the Orlando Magic, which he cofounded in 1987 and helped lead to the NBA finals in 1995 and 2009. Twenty-three of his teams have gone to the NBA playoffs and five have made the NBA finals. In 1996, Pat was named as one of the 50 most influential people in NBA history by a national publication.

Pat has been an integral part of NBA history, including bringing the NBA to Orlando. He has traded Pete Maravich as well as traded for Julius Erving, Moses Malone, and Penny Hardaway, and he has won four NBA draft lotteries, including back-to-back winners in 1992 and 1993. He also drafted Charles Barkley, Shaquille O'Neal, Maurice Cheeks, Andrew Toney, and Darryl Dawkins. He signed Billy Cunningham, Chuck Daly, and Matt Guokas to their first professional coaching contracts. Nineteen of his former players have become NBA head coaches, nine have become college head coaches, while seven have become assistant NBA coaches.

Pat and his wife, Ruth, are the parents of 19 children, including 14 adopted from four nations, ranging in age from 28 to 42. For one year, 16 of his children were all teenagers at the same time. He and Ruth have 14 grandchildren. Pat and his family have been featured in *Sports Illustrated, Reader's Digest, Good Housekeeping, Family Circle, The Wall Street Journal, Focus on the Family, New Man Magazine*, plus all of the major television networks, "The Maury Povich Show," and Dr. Robert Schuller's *Hour of Power*.

Pat teaches an adult Sunday school class at First Baptist Church of Orlando and hosts three weekly radio shows. From 1996 to 2011, he completed 58 marathons— including the Boston Marathon 13 times—and also climbed Mt. Rainier. He is a weight lifter, Civil War buff, and serious baseball fan. Every winter he plays in Major League Fantasy Camps and has caught Hall of Famers Bob Feller, Bob Gibson, Fergie Jenkins, Bert Blyleven, Rollie Fingers, Gaylord Perry, Phil Niekro, Tom Seaver, and Goose Gossage.

Pat was raised in Wilmington, Delaware, earned his bachelor's degree at Wake Forest University, and his master's degree at Indiana University. He is a member of the Wake Forest Sports Hall of Fame after catching for the Demon Deacon baseball team, including the 1962 Atlantic Coast Conference championship team. He is also a member of the Delaware Sports Hall of Fame.

Contact Pat Williams at:
Pat Williams
c/o Orlando Magic
8701 Maitland Summit Boulevard
Orlando, FL 32810
Phone: 407-916-2404
pwilliams@orlandomagic.com

Visit Pat Williams' website at: www.patwilliamsmotivate.com
On Twitter: @OrlandoMagicPat

If you would like to set up a speaking engagement for Pat Williams, please write or call his assistant, Andrew Herdliska, at the previous address, or at 407-916-2401. Requests can also be faxed to 407-916-2986 or e-mailed to aherdliska@orlandomagic.com

We would love to hear from you. Please send your comments about this book to Pat Williams at the previous address. Thank you.